# Niagara Falls Ontario Book 2 in Colour Photos, Saving Our History One Photo at a Time

Photography
by Barbara Raué
©2021

Series Name: Cruising Ontario

Book 208: Niagara Falls Book 2

Cover photo: Zimmerman Avenue Bank, Page 31

©2021 All the photos in this book have been taken with my cameras. I own the rights to them.

# Series Name: Cruising Ontario
# Saving Our History One Photo at a Time
# in colour photos

Books Available in Alphabetical Order:
Aberfoyle, Acton, Ajax, Alton, Amherstburg, Ancaster, Arthur, Auburn, Aylmer, Ayr, Beaver Valley, Belgrave, Belleville, Bloomingdale, Blyth, Brantford, Brockville, Burford, Burlington, Caledon, Caledonia, Cambridge, Carlow, Chatsworth, Clifford, Collingwood, Conestogo, Delhi, Dorchester to Aylmer, Drayton, Drumbo, Dundas, Dunlop, Eden Mills, Elmira, Elora, Erin, Essex, Fergus, Goderich, Grimsby, Guelph, Hagersville, Hamilton, Hanover, Harriston, Hespeler, Jarvis, Kingston, Kingsville, Kitchener, Lake Superior, Lincoln, Linwood, Listowel, London, Lucknow, Merrickville, Mono, Mount Forest, Mount Pleasant, Neustadt, New Hamburg, Newboro, Newport, Niagara-on-the-Lake, Oakville, Onondaga, Orangeville, Orillia, Oshawa, Owen Sound, Palmerston, Paris, Pelham, Perth, Peterborough, Petrolia, Pickering, Port Colborne, Port Elgin, Portland, Preston, Rockwood, Sarnia, Sault Ste. Marie, Seaforth, Sheffield, Shelburne, Simcoe, Smiths Falls, Smithville, Southampton, St. Catharines, St. George, St. Jacobs, St. Marys, St. Thomas, Stoney Creek, Stratford, Thamesford, Thunder Bay, Tillsonburg, Toronto, Waterdown, Waterford, Waterloo, Welland, Wellesley, West Flamborough, Westport, Whitby, Windsor, Wingham, Woodstock

Book 201-202: Whitby
Book 203: Ajax, Pickering
Book 204-206: Oshawa
Book 207-209: Niagara Falls

## Table of Contents

| | |
|---|---|
| Dunn Street | Page 5 |
| Bridge Street | Page 7 |
| Queen Street | Page 9 |
| Erie Avenue | Page 24 |
| Simcoe Street | Page 26 |
| Zimmerman Avenue | Page 31 |
| Fourth Avenue | Page 40 |
| Third Avenue | Page 41 |
| Ellis Street | Page 42 |
| Morrison Street | Page 44 |
| Ontario Avenue | Page 47 |
| River Road | Page 49 |
| Bampfield Street | Page 67 |

Niagara Falls Ontario is located along the Niagara Gorge on the western bank of the Niagara River which flows from Lake Erie to Lake Ontario. The Niagara River flows over Niagara Falls at this location and creates a natural spectacle that attracts millions of tourists each year.

In 1853 construction began to build an international suspension bridge over the Niagara Gorge. This brought work and prosperity to the north end of Stamford Township. A shanty-town development was erected to house workers at the base of the bridge. Over the years this became the Village of Elgin. Amalgamation of the Village of Elgin with the Town of Clifton was caused by the economic impact of the Great Western, Erie and Ontario Railways. The prosperous town boasted fifteen grocery stores and twenty saloons and hotels.

Samuel Zimmerman, one of the founding fathers of the city, came from Pennsylvania in 1842 with lots of ambition, and some knowledge of construction. He rebuilt parts of the Welland Canal. Recognizing the importance of railroads, Zimmerman began building railway lines including the Great Western (now Canadian National) from Hamilton. Zimmerman's company played a role in building the Railway Suspension Bridge across the Niagara River Gorge.

During Zimmerman's lifetime, there were four small communities within what is now Niagara Falls: Chippawa to the south, Clifton, Drummondville, and Stamford Village in the north.

The majority of the early downtown businesses were located on the lower part of Bridge Street, Erie Avenue and River Road, with a few businesses on Clifton Avenue (now Zimmerman) and Park Street. At the turn of the century, retail activity slowly started to shift to Queen Street where to date some of these firms are still operating. The residences of Queen Street have given way to stores and offices that form the Downtown core we see today.

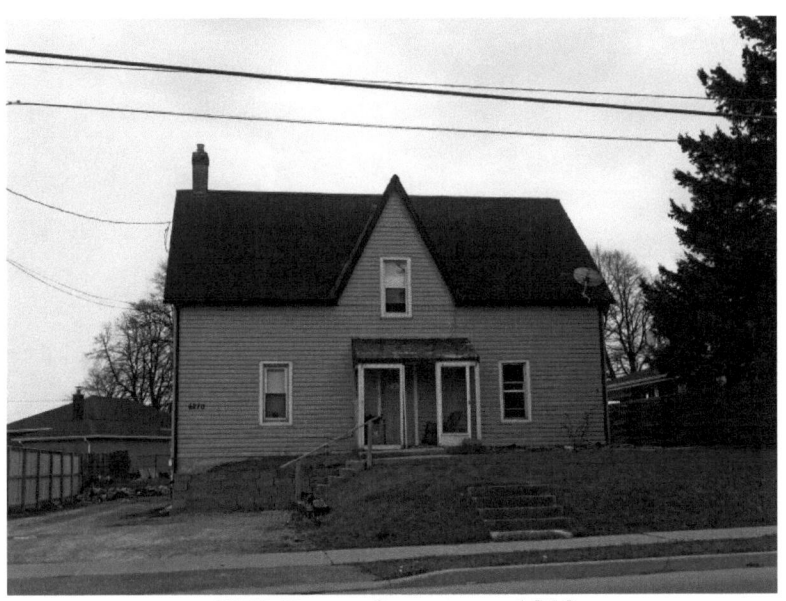

6270 Dunn Street – c. 1812

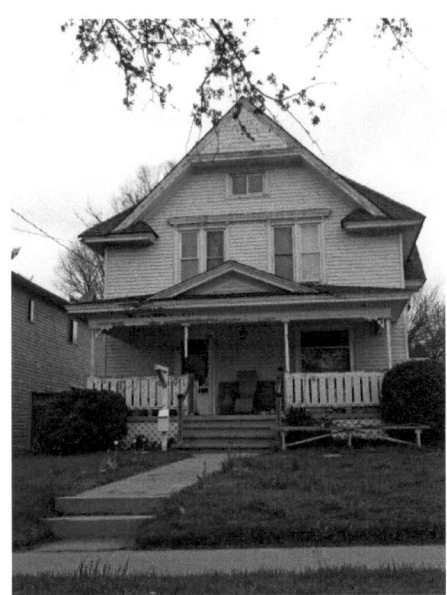

6491 Dunn Street

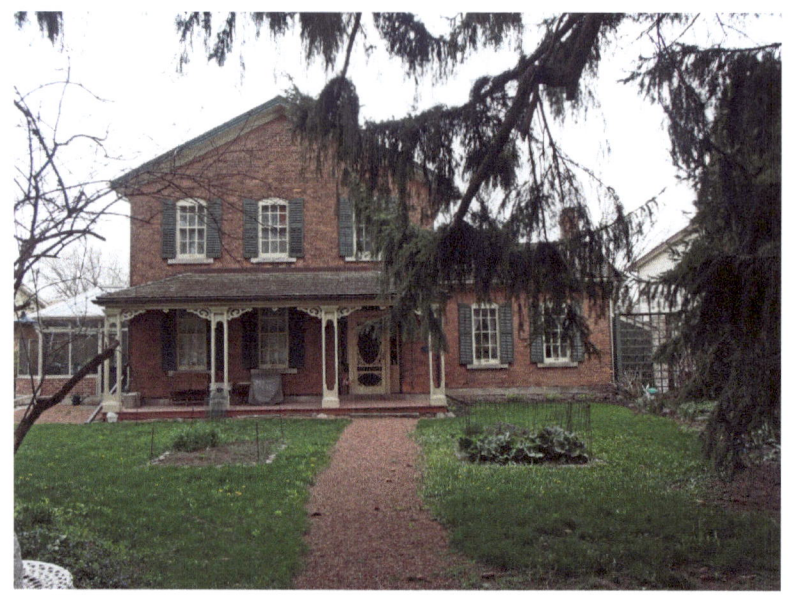

6590 Dunn Street - Stamford Township Lot 161 was first obtained from the Crown by Haggai Skinner who likely built the earlier cabin. It was Henry Spence's farm from 1854 to 1885. Mr. Spence came from England in 1834 and was noted for his fine brickwork. In 1893, the house and property were purchased by David Weaver and remained in the Weaver family until 1973.

The larger front section of the house was constructed by Drummondville Mason Henry Spence, while the rear wood frame wing was originally a settler's cabin dating to around 1800. An old brick scullery is also attached to the west side of the cabin and has remnants of an original cauldron and bread oven. A board and batten garage was added to the rear by the current owners.

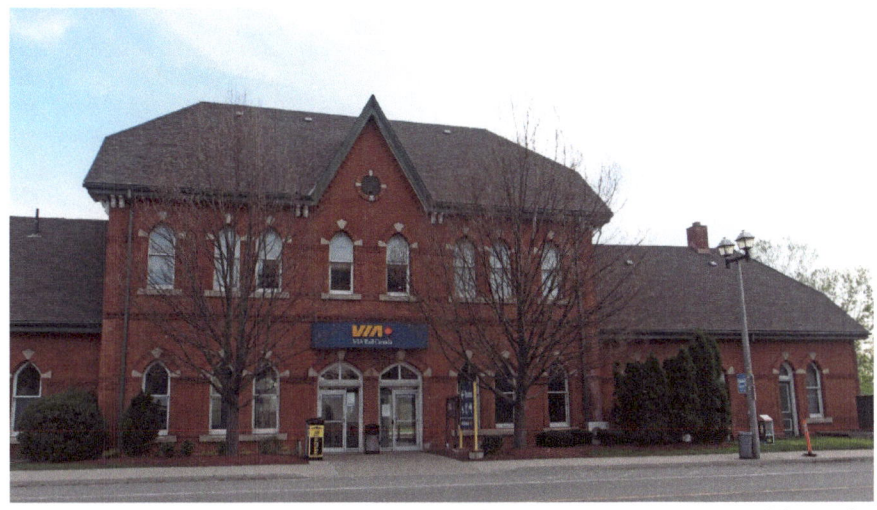

4267 Bridge Street - Via Rail Station - Positioned beside the International Railway Bridge, this was the busiest and most prestigious terminal of the Great Western and Grand Trunk Railroads. It serviced the growing tourist trade, and was a popular social center with a restaurant in the east wing.

Constructed in the Gothic Revival style favored for rail depots of the Victorian age, it has a hipped gable roof, decorative brick banding and limestone door and window accents. Originally installed in the gable ends were carved bargeboards.

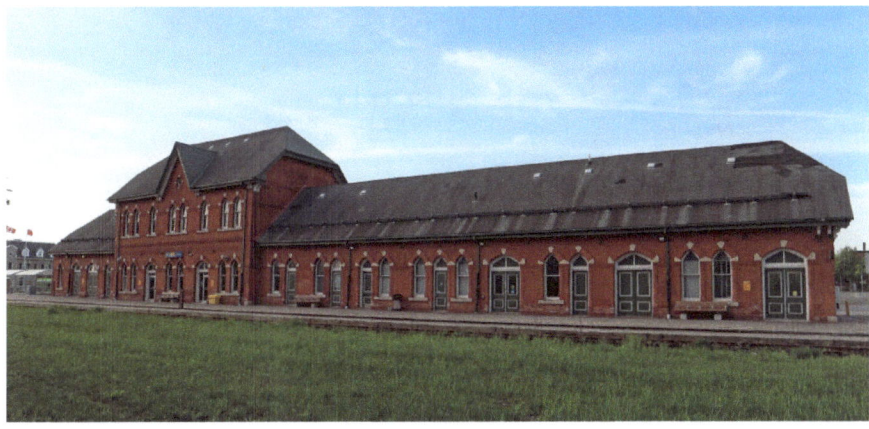

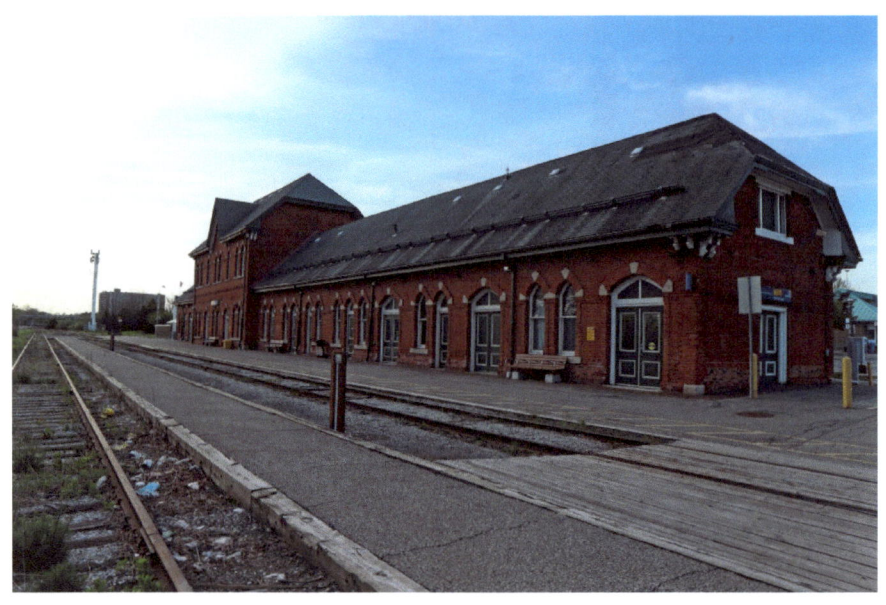

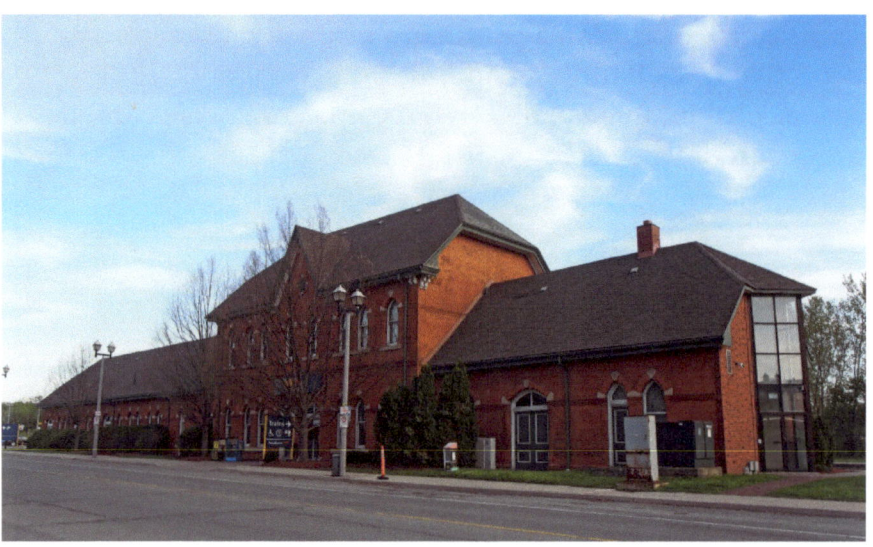

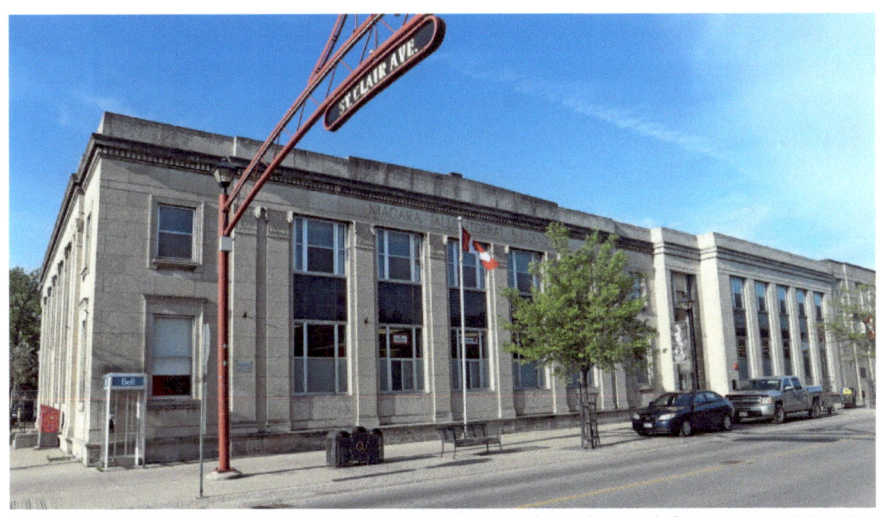

4500 Queen Street – Niagara Falls Federal Building – 1930 - Its art deco facade has a simplified cornice; the windows are separated vertically by squared pilasters with ionic capitals and broken horizontally by stone panels.

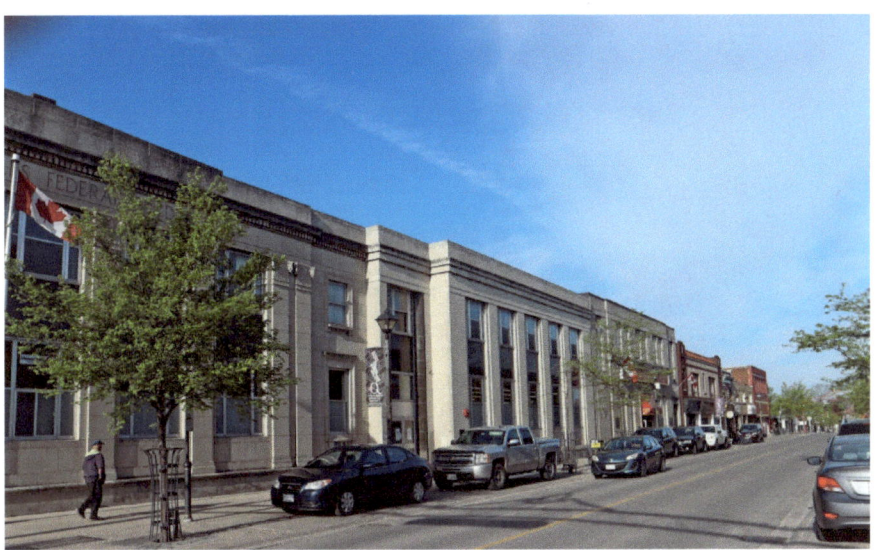

Queen Street

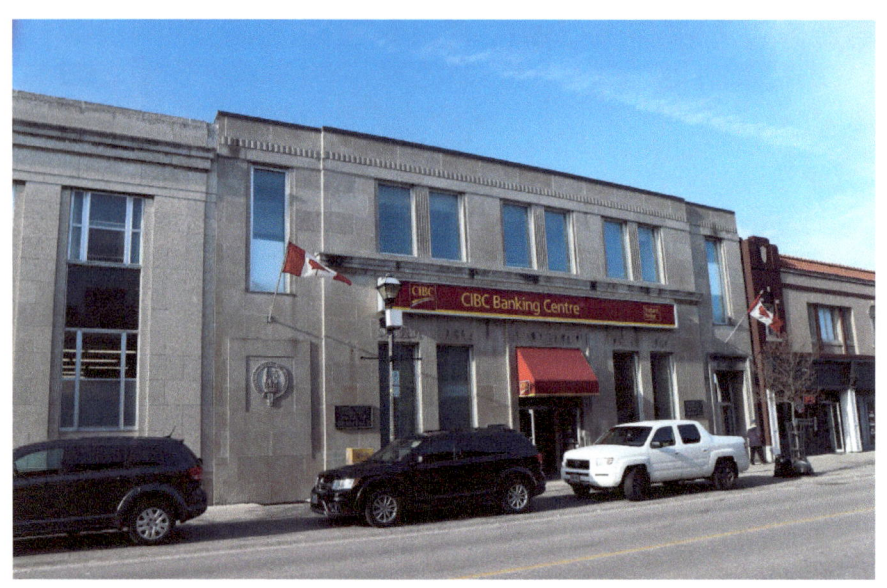

Queen Street

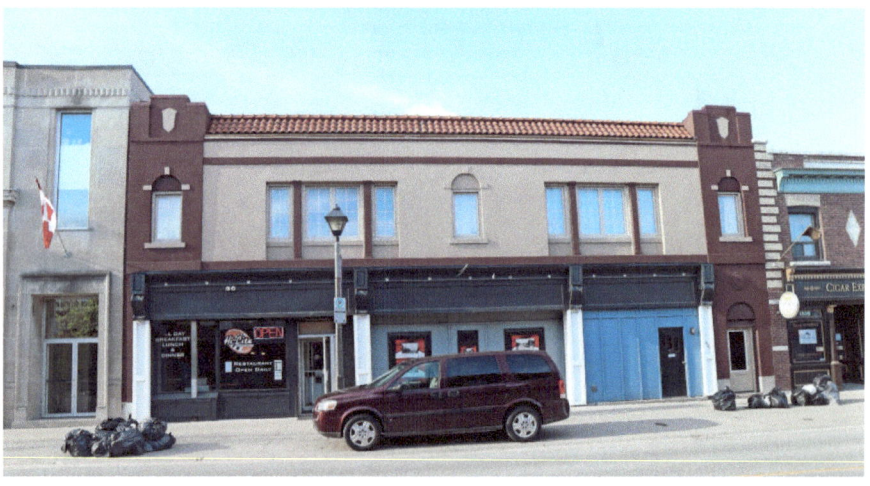

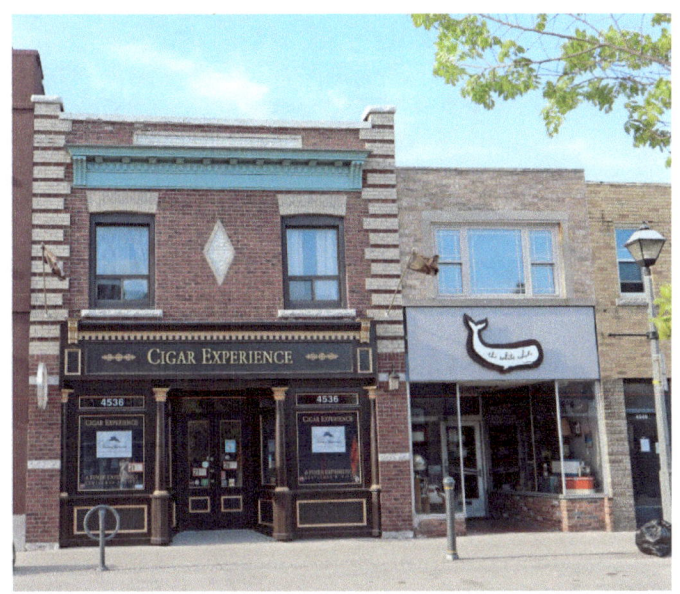

4636 Queen Street

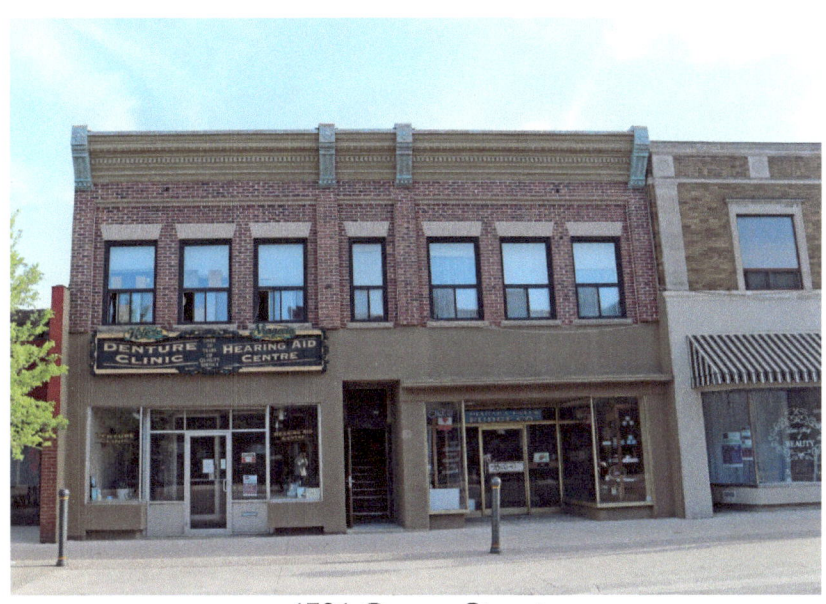

4531 Queen Street

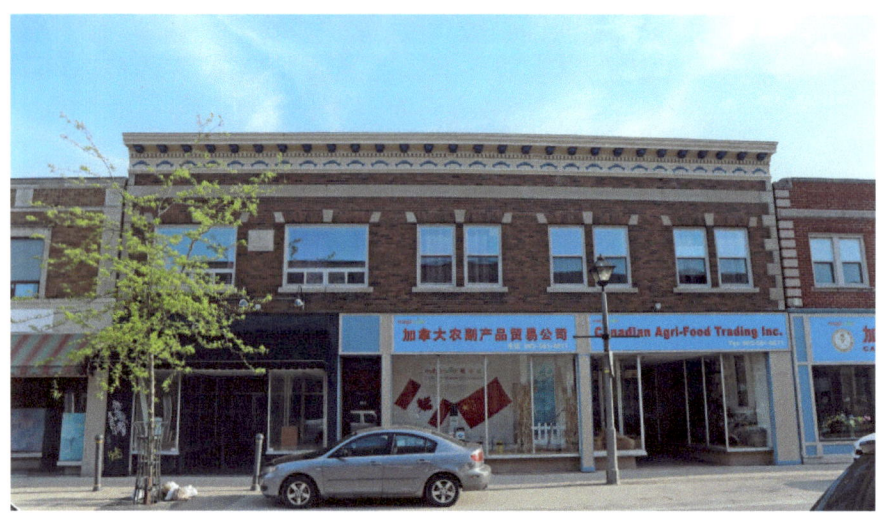

4511 Queen Street

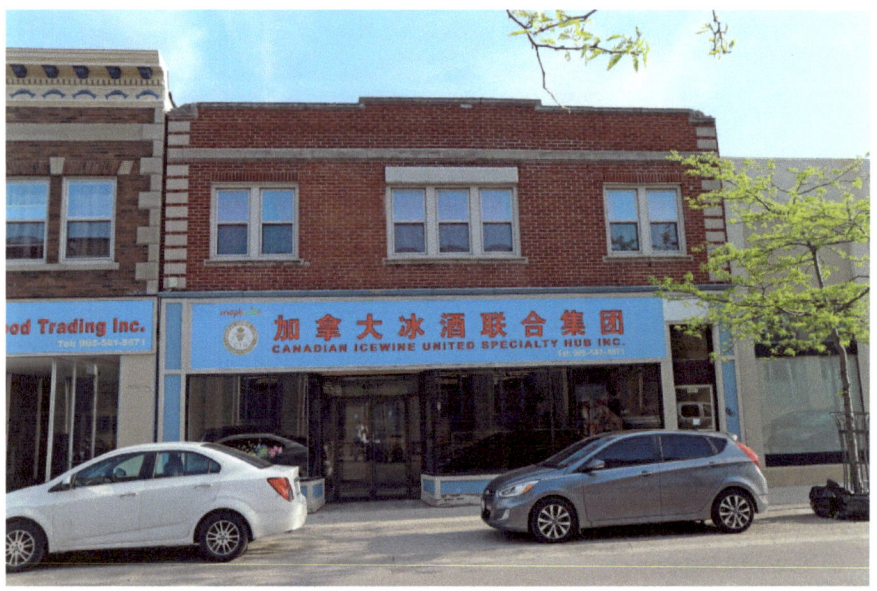

4501 Queen Street

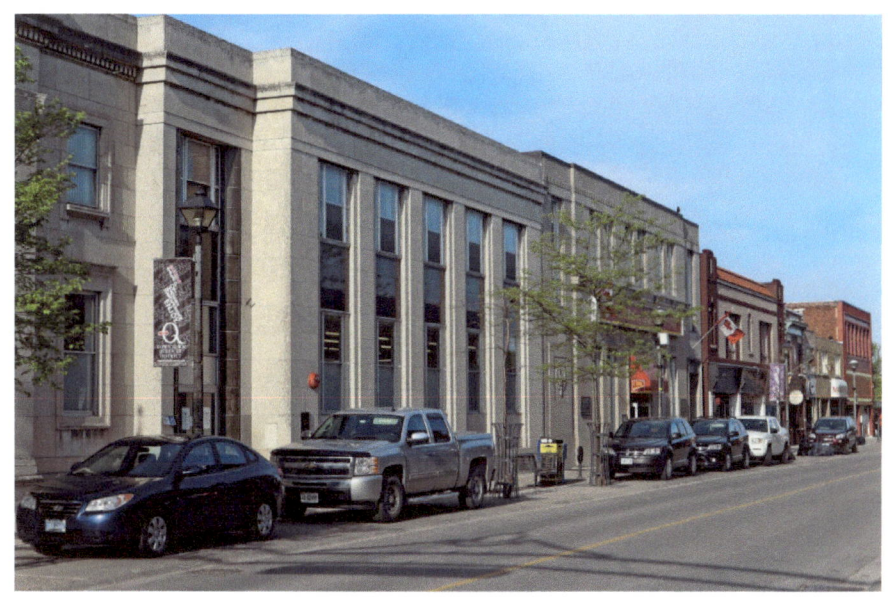

Queen Street

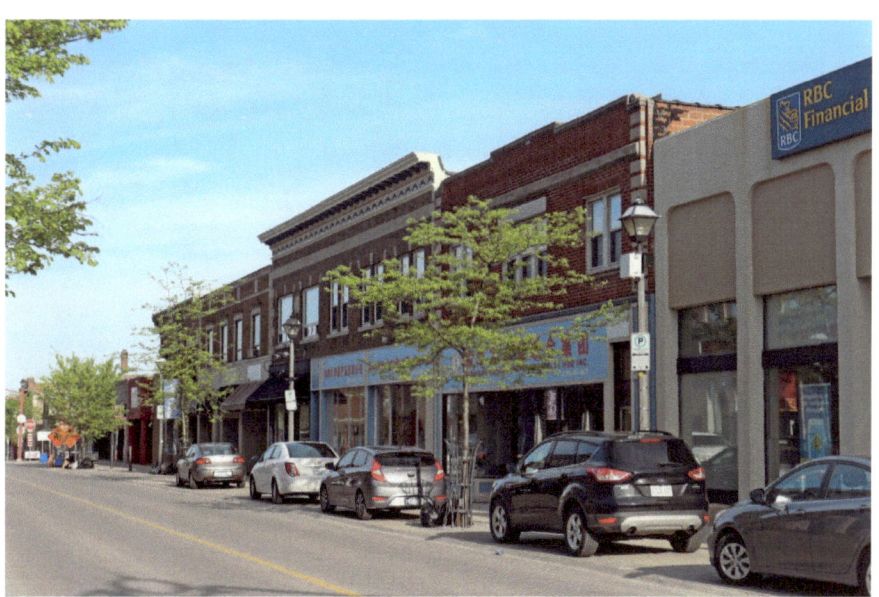

Queen Street

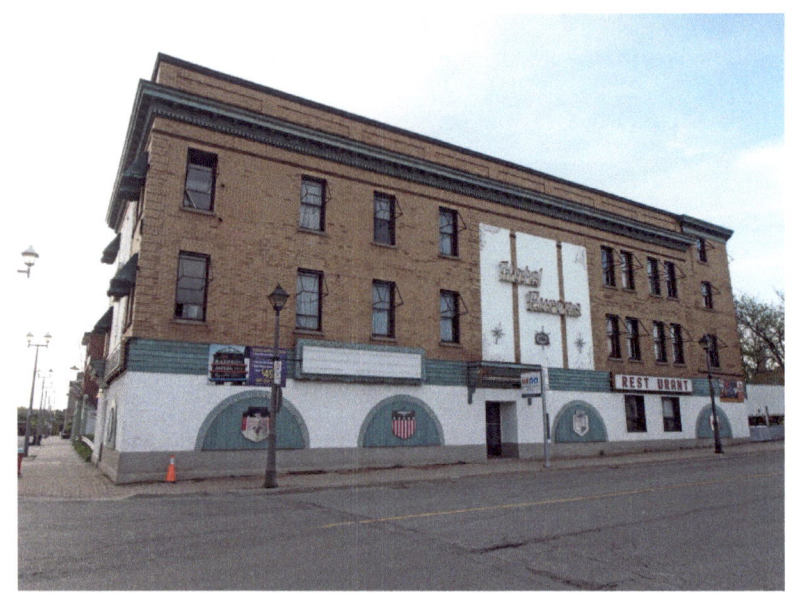

4337 Queen Street – Hotel Europa - 1910

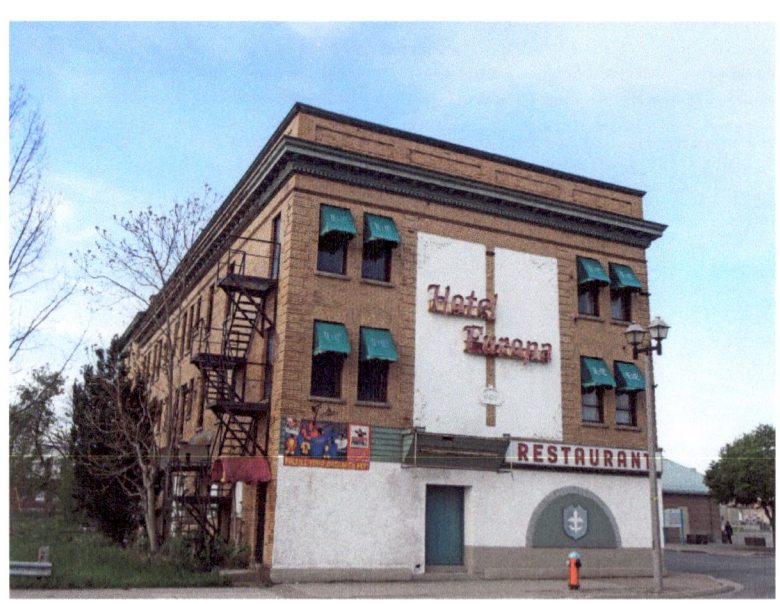

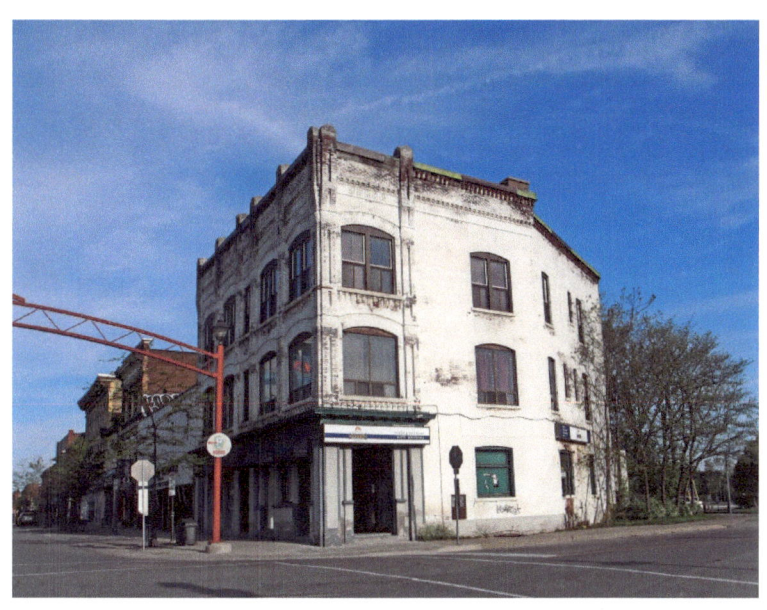

4299 Queen Street – 1894 – former Bank of Hamilton

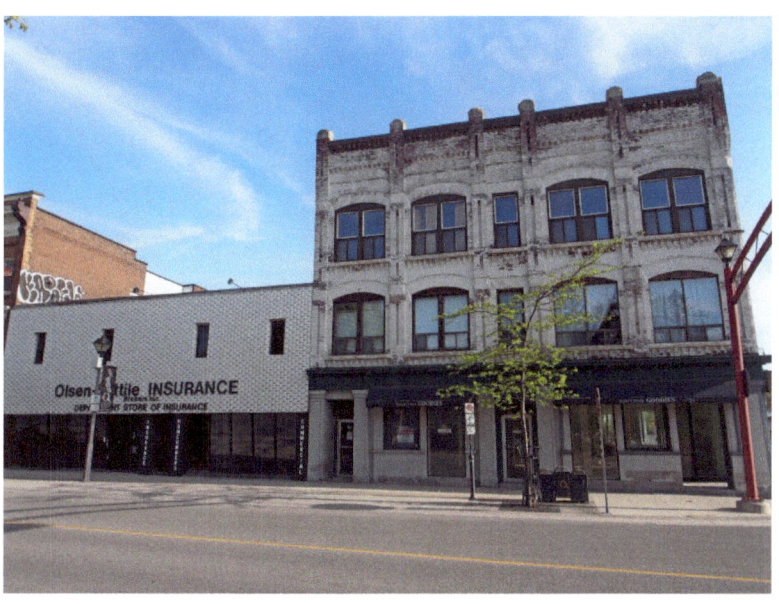

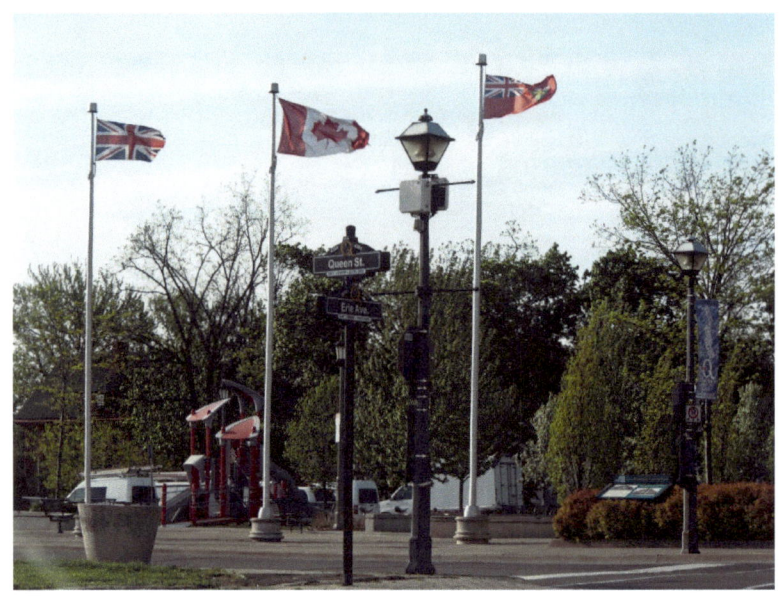

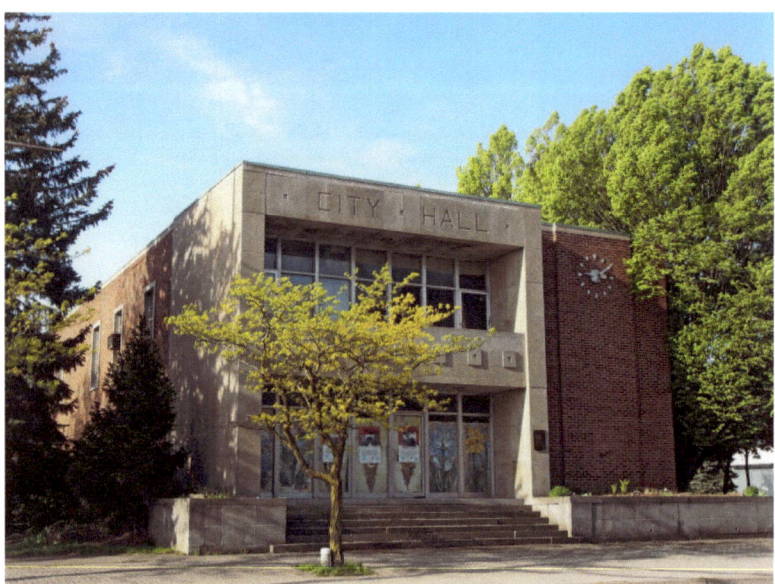

4310 Queen Street – City Hall – 1866 – For years there was a small balcony over the front entrance and orators spoke to the crowds gathered below. It served as City Hall for Niagara Falls until the new building opened in May 1970.

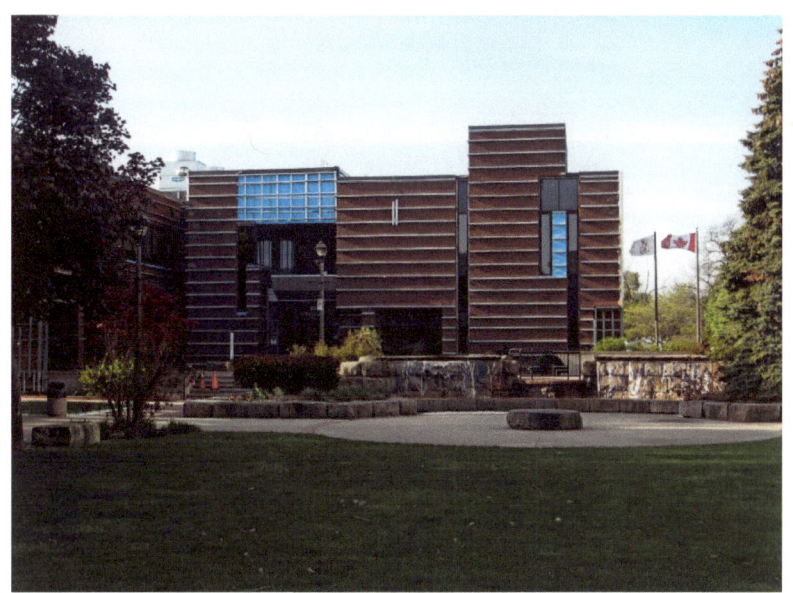

New City Hall

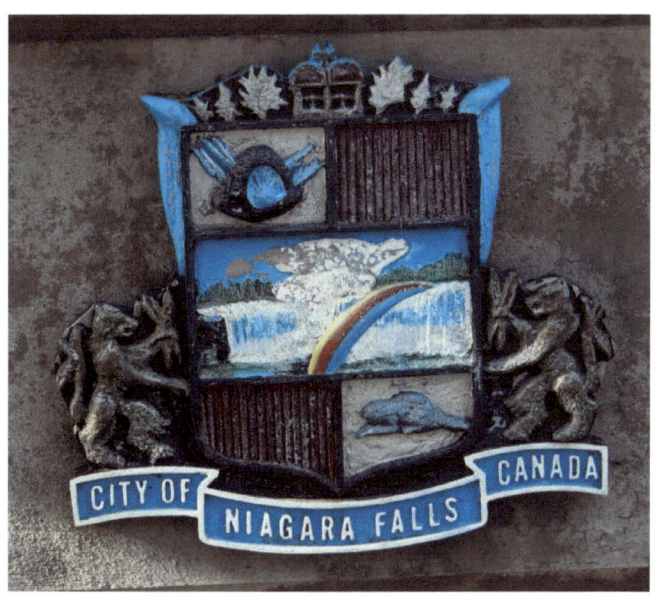

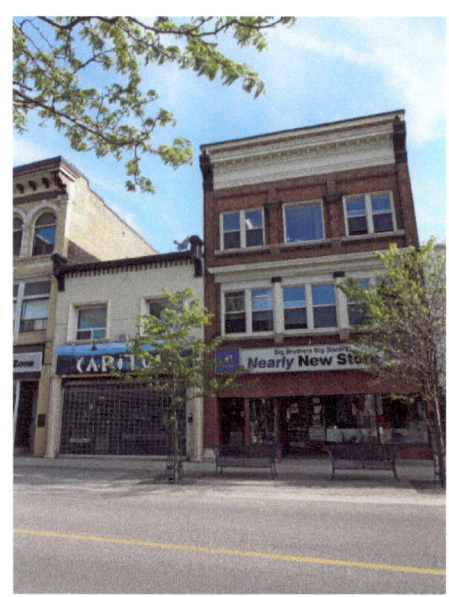

4311-4313 Queen Street

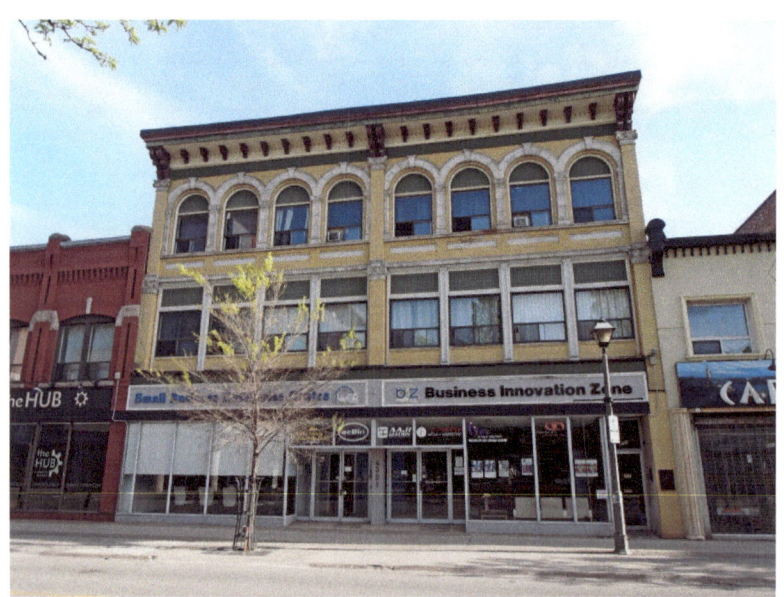

4321 Queen Street

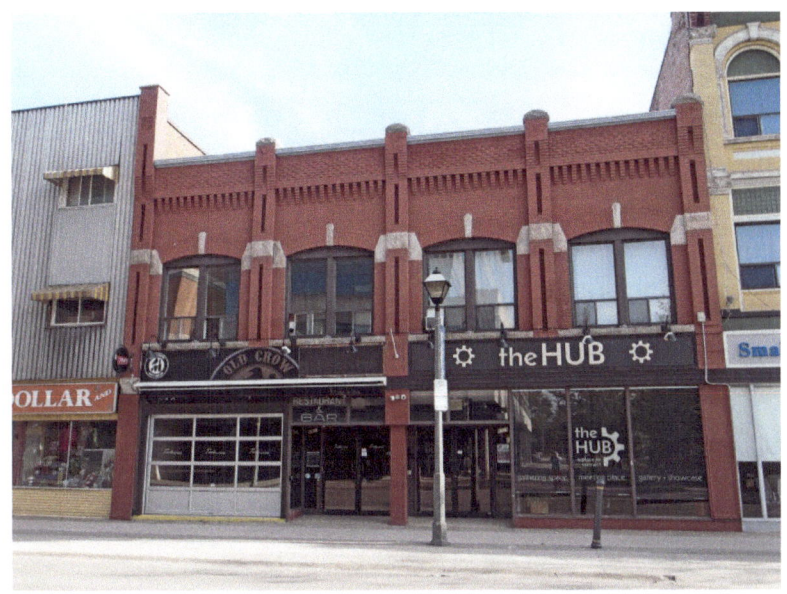

4333-4337 Queen Street

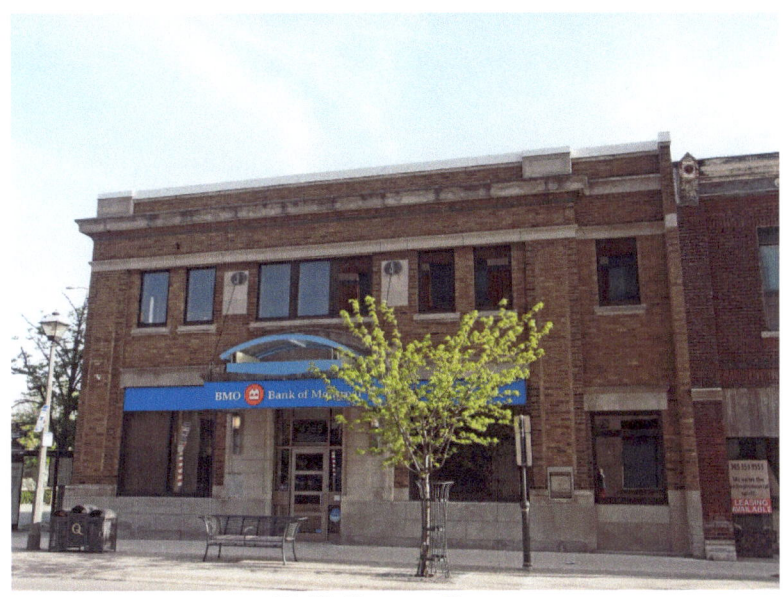

4365 Queen Street

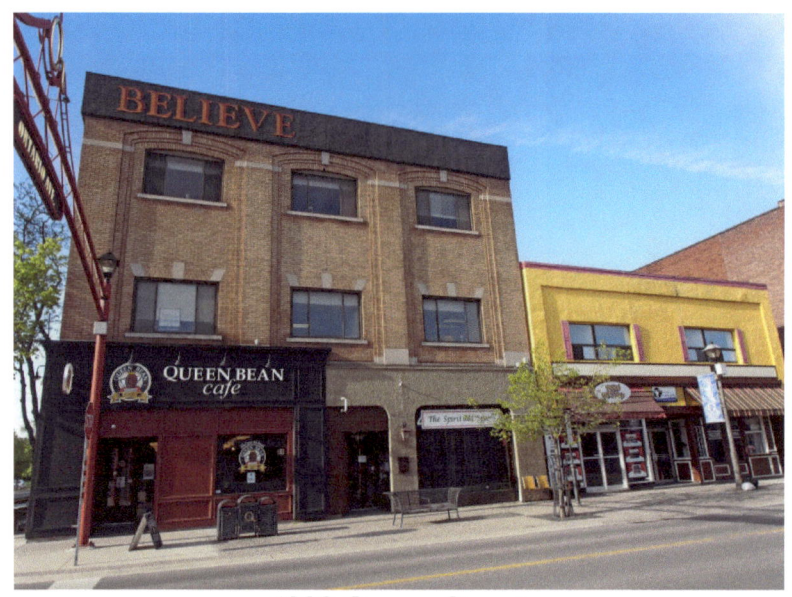

4388 Queen Street

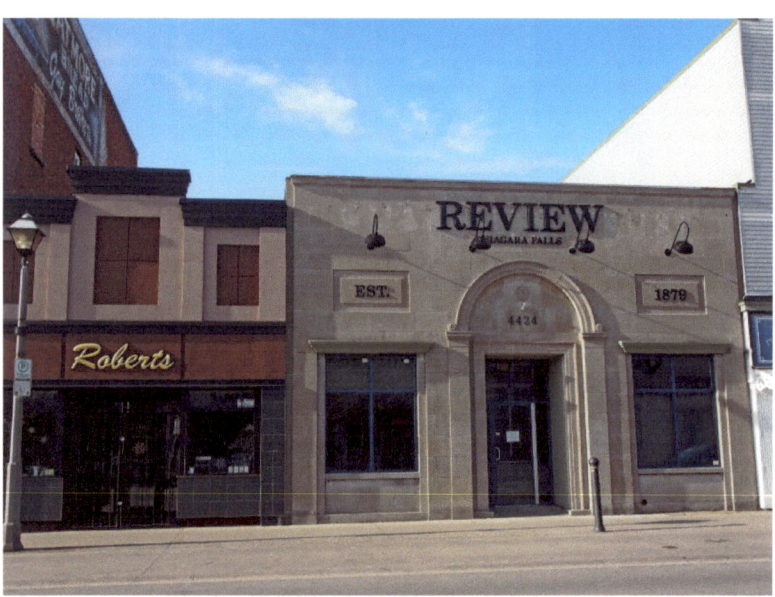

4424 Queen Street – Niagara Falls Review – established 1879

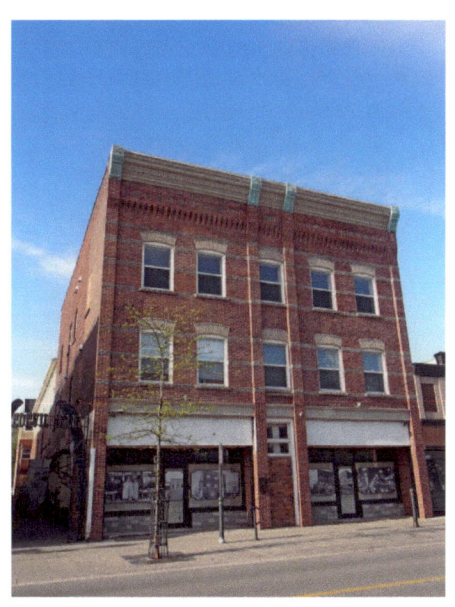

4416 Queen Street

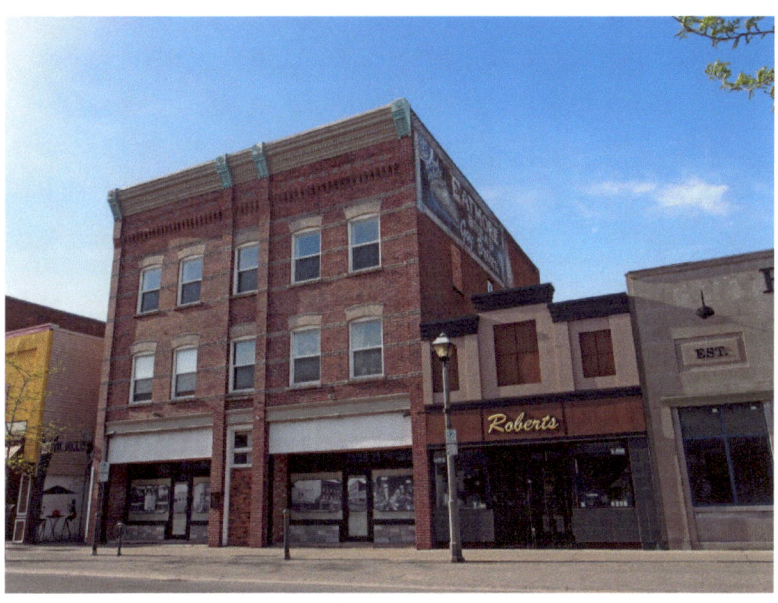

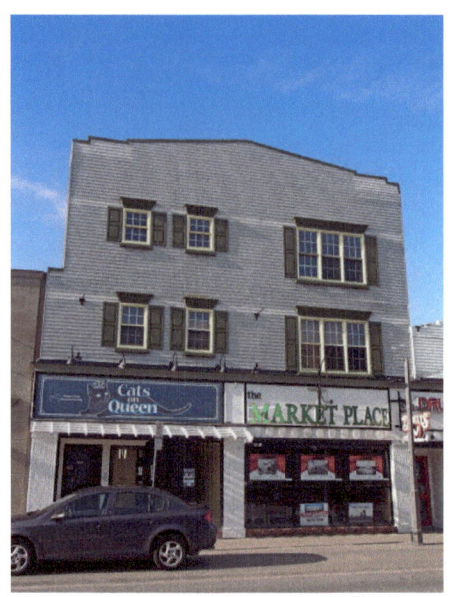

4426 Queen Street

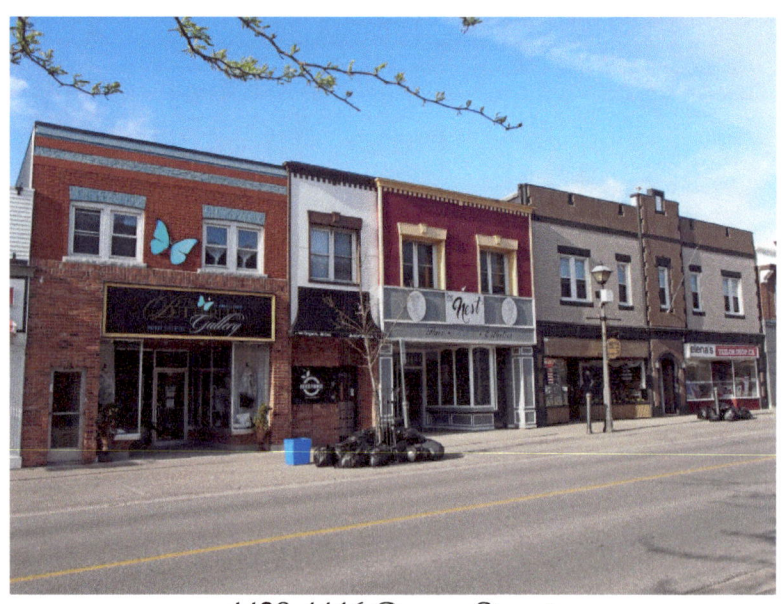

4438-4446 Queen Street

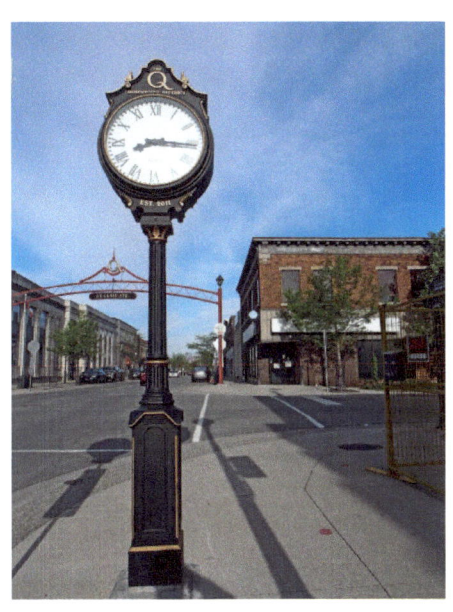

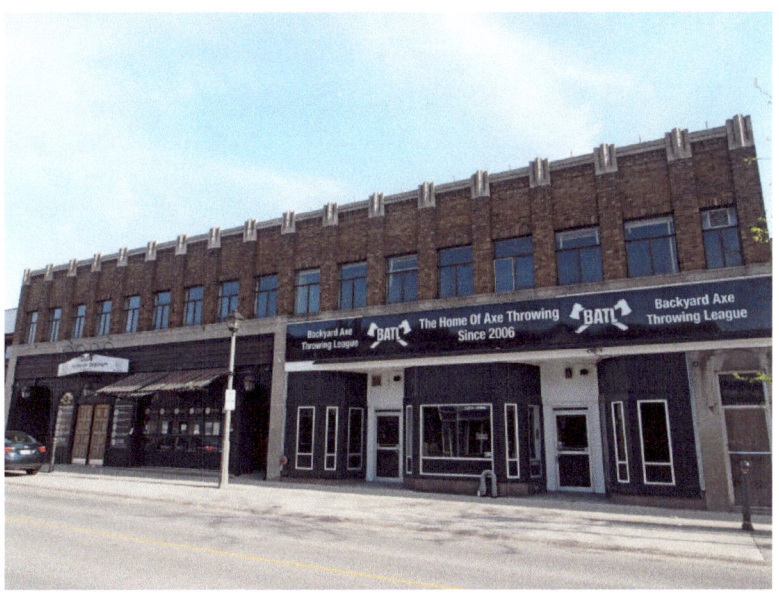

4437 Queen Street

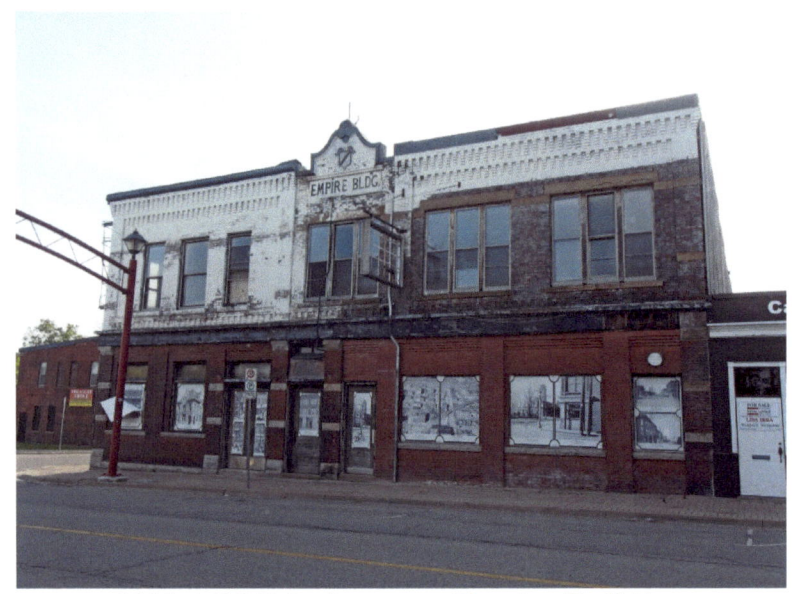

4600-4610 Erie Avenue – Empire Building

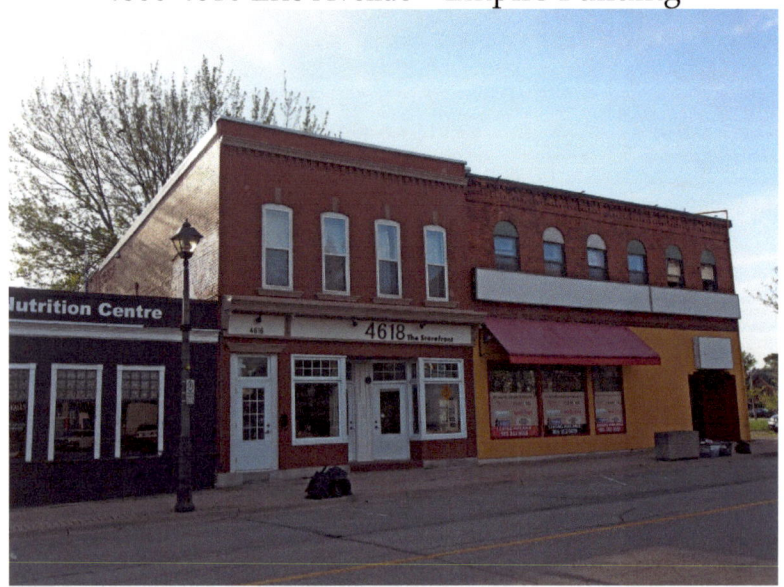

4616-4624 Erie Avenue - #4624 housed the hardware store operated by the Clark-Pattinson family from 1885 until it closed in 1976. A workshop with skilled tradesmen once occupied the second floor.

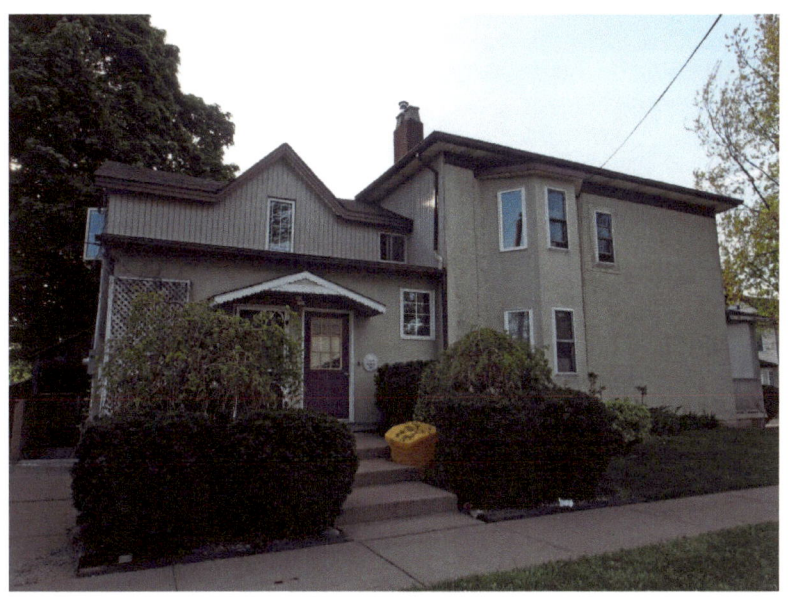

Erie Avenue

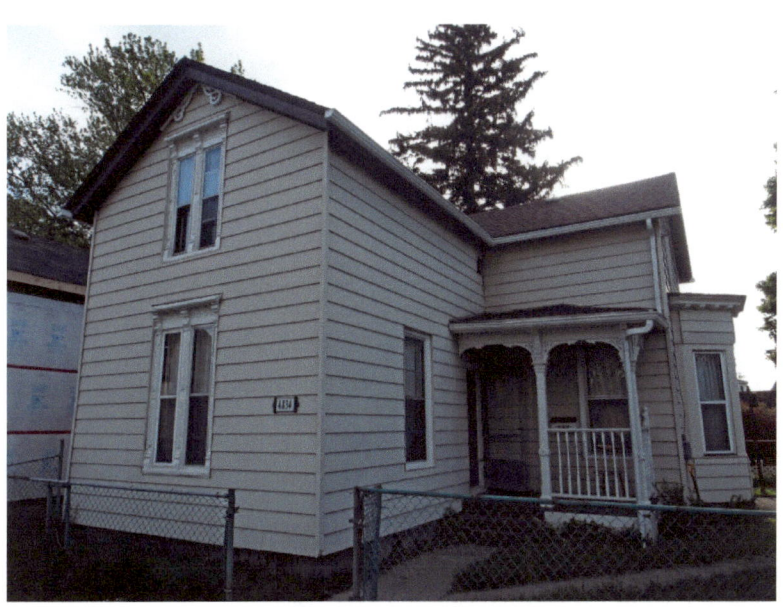

4834 Erie Avenue

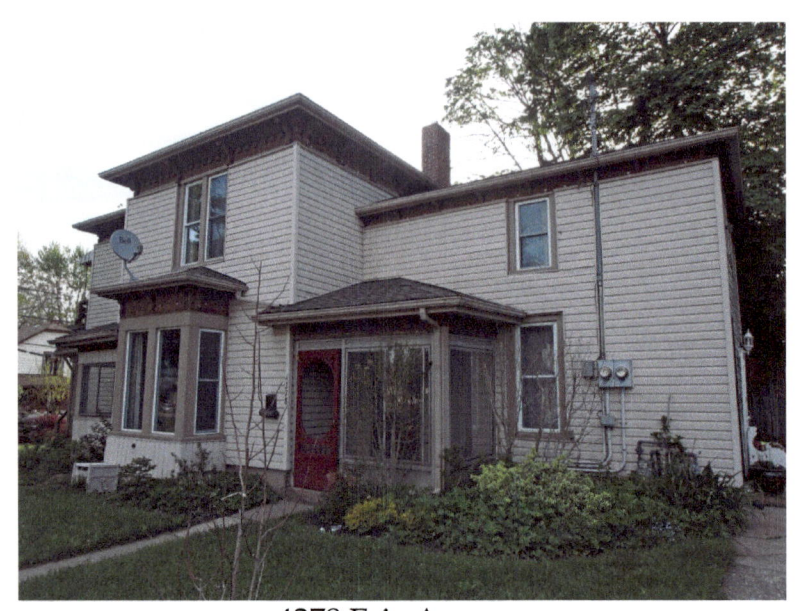

4278 Erie Avenue

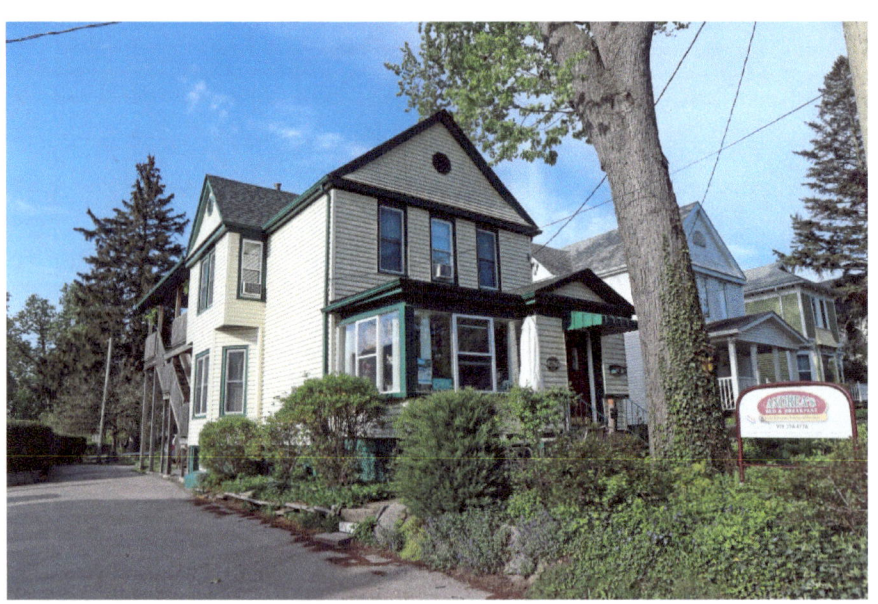

4286 Simcoe Street – Andrea's Bed and Breakfast

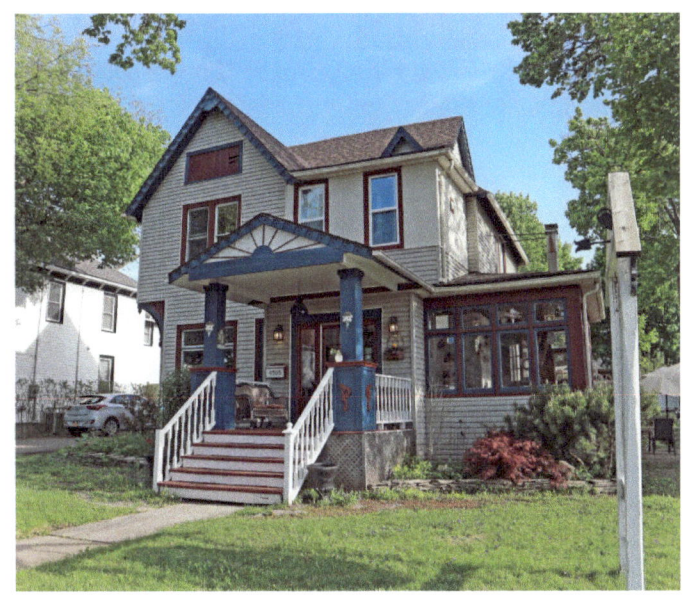

4305 Simcoe Street

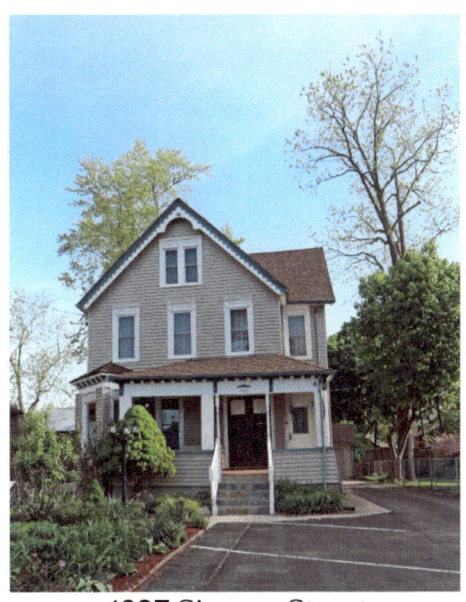

4327 Simcoe Street

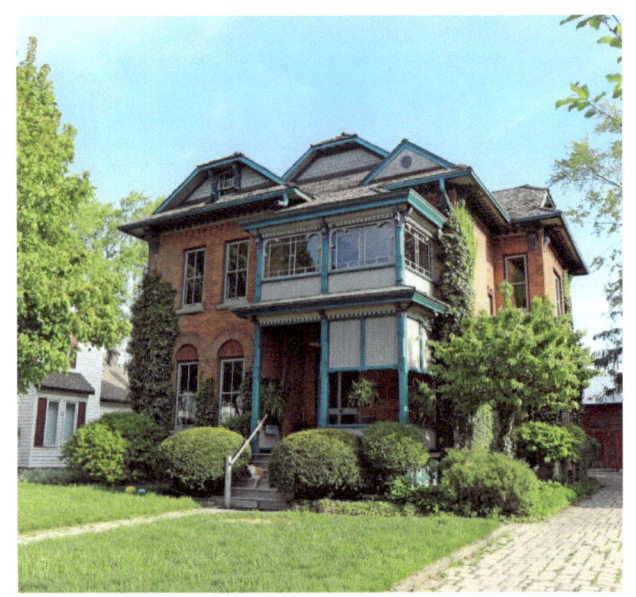

4337 Simcoe Street

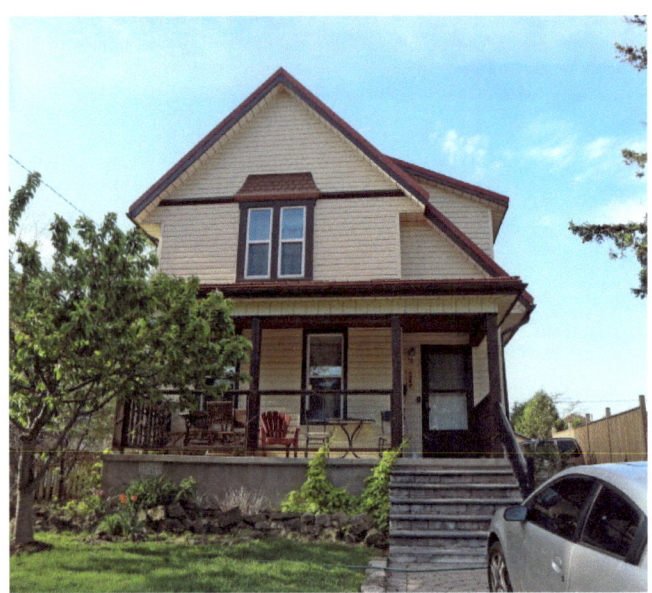

4340 Simcoe Street

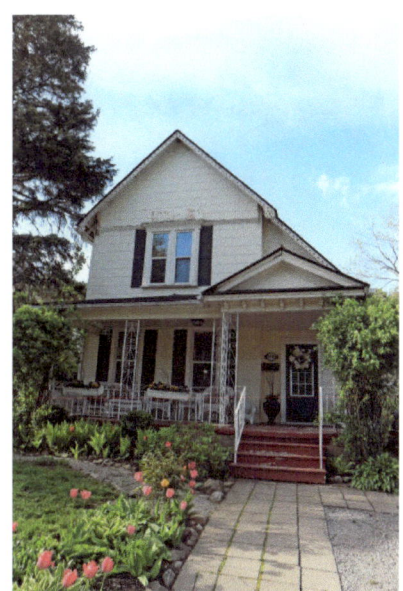

4310 Simcoe Street

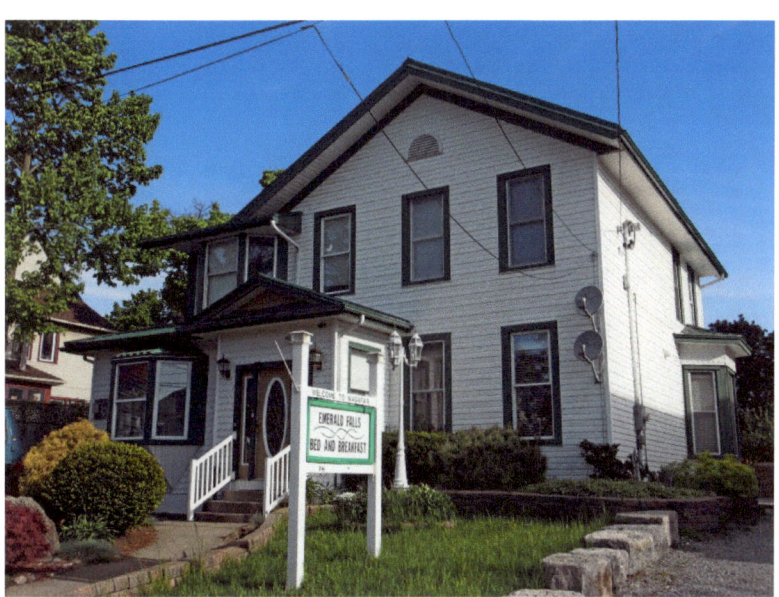

4291 Simcoe Street - Emerald Falls Bed and Breakfast

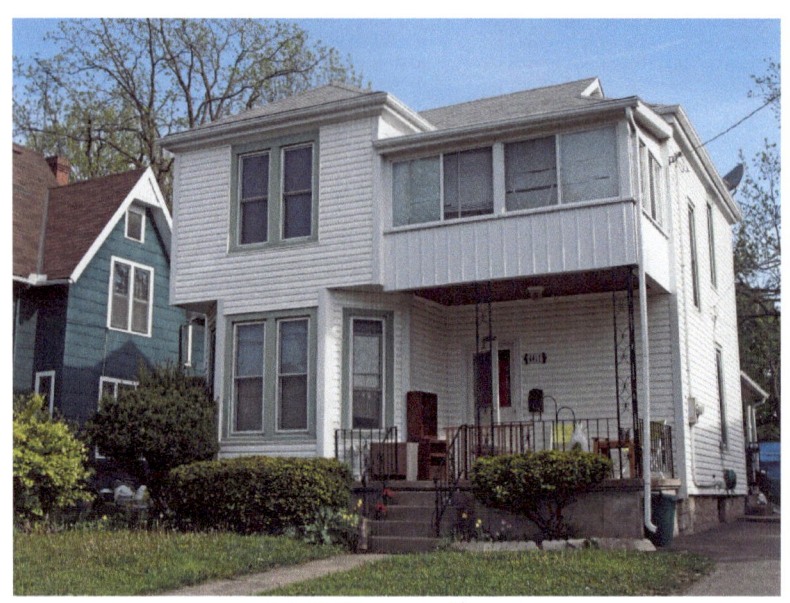

4417 Simcoe Street

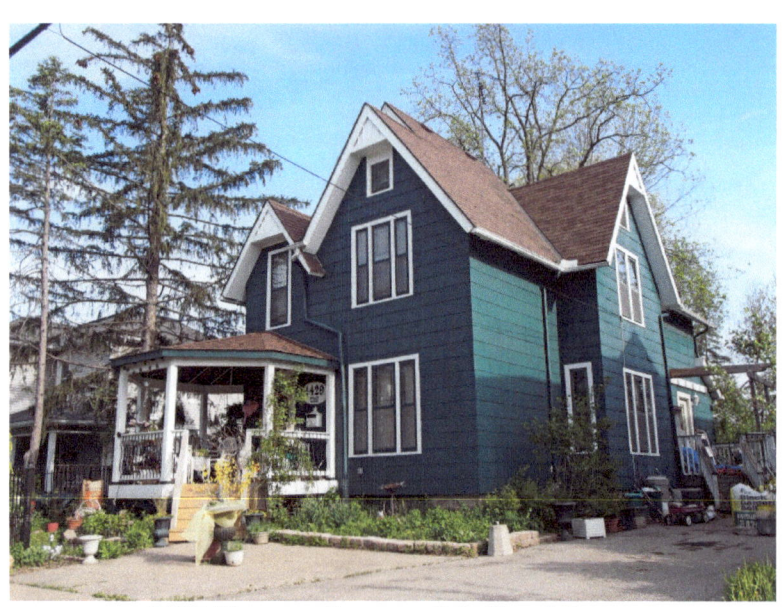

4429 Simcoe Street – Mulley Manor

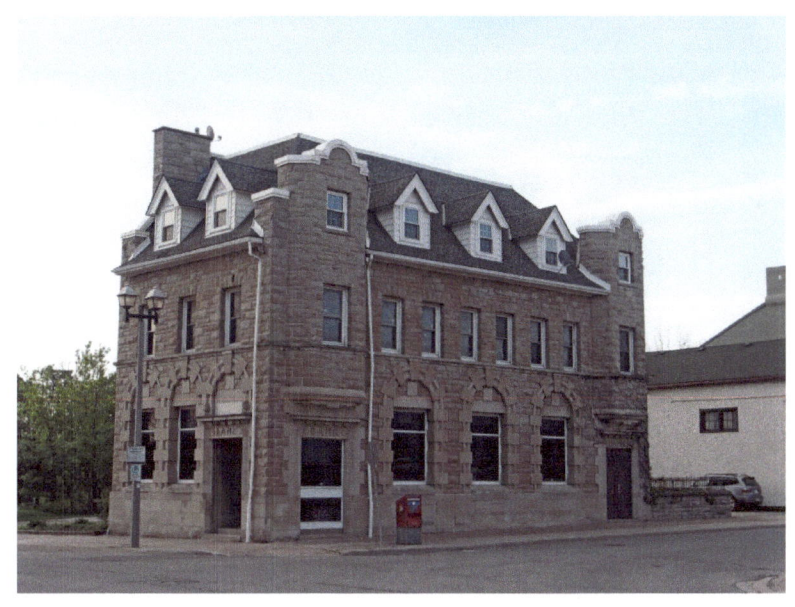

Zimmerman Avenue - Bank

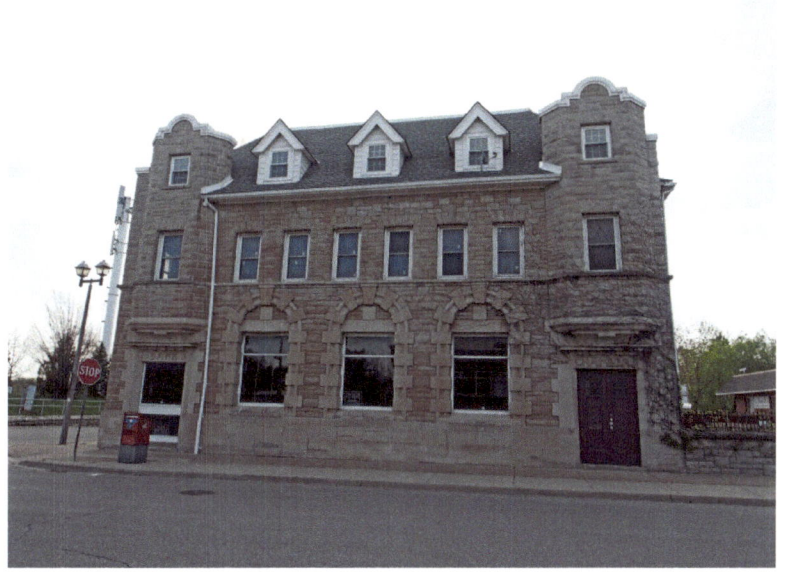

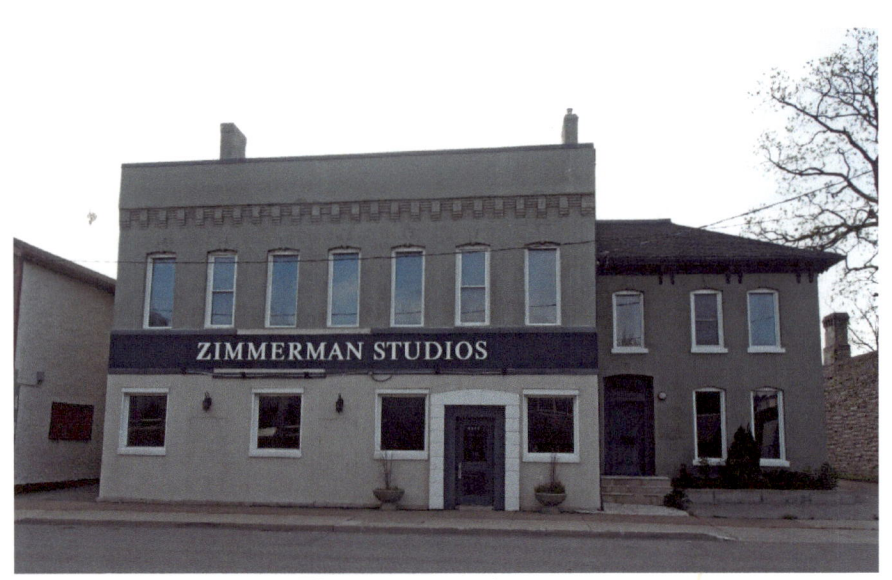

Zimmerman Avenue

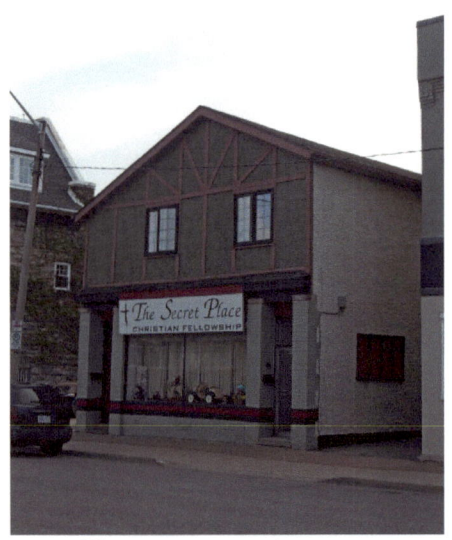

Zimmerman Avenue

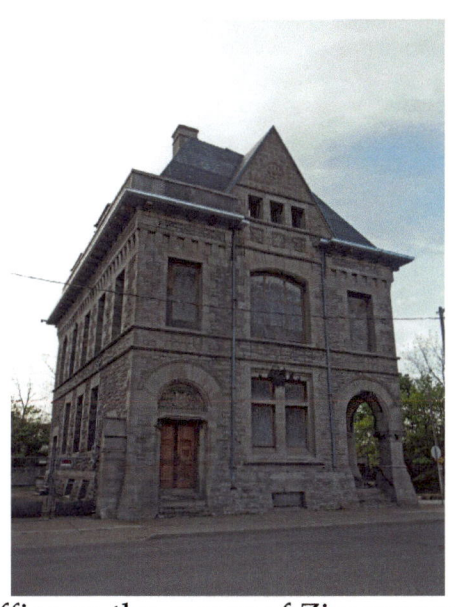

The old post office on the corner of Zimmerman Avenue and Park Street

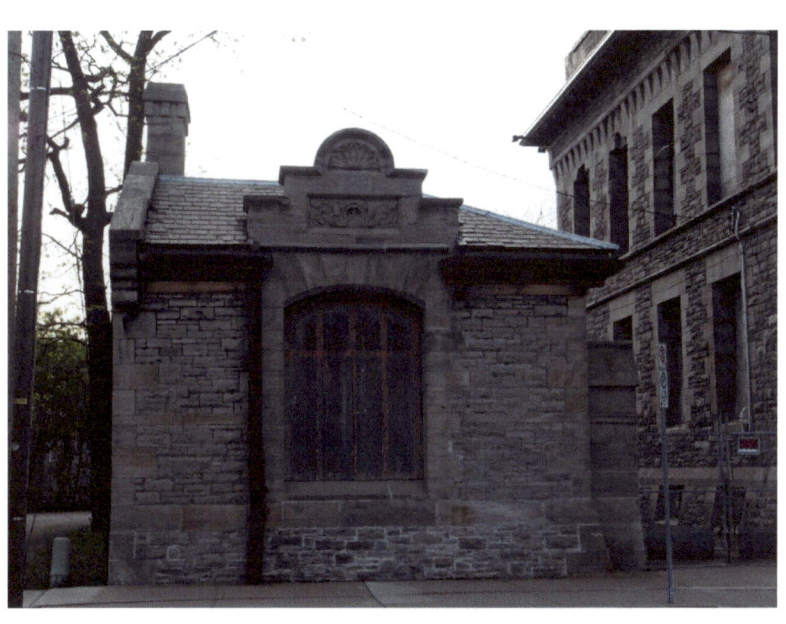

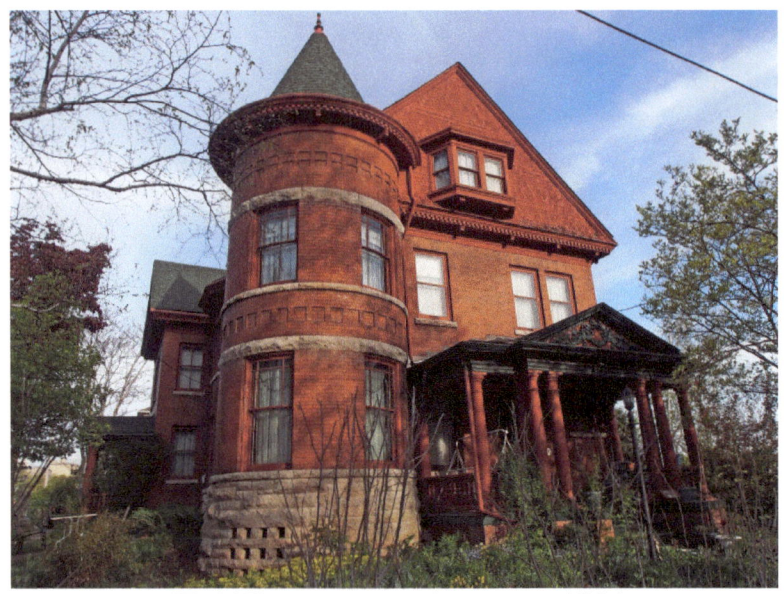

4711 Zimmerman Avenue - 1896

The house served as both the home and office of Dr. James McGarry, and later that of his son, pediatrician Dr. Howard McGarry. Between them, the house was the center of medical care for families in Niagara Falls over the course of nearly ninety years.

The home has a corner tower, pressed brick and limestone exterior, and irregular roofline. The large Neo-Classical front porch has rounded columns, frieze and a decorated closed pediment. A surgery was added to the rear of the house in 1905.

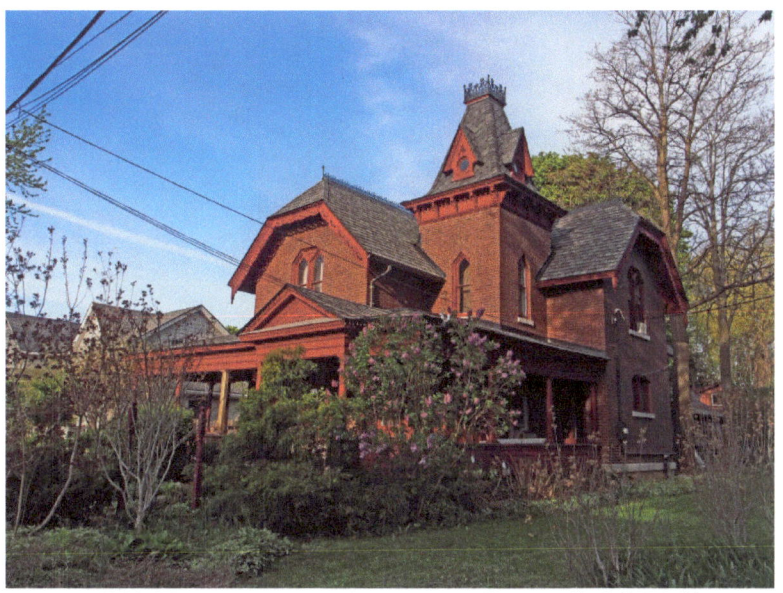

4761 Zimmerman Avenue – Bampfield Hall

    James Bampfield built this second home for his wife Margaret who apparently never liked their first house. For generations it remained the property of the Bampfields as they rose to become one of the most prominent commercial families in Niagara Falls.

    The house is built primarily in the Gothic Revival style with pointed windows, a jerkinhead roof, and gingerbread trim in the gable ends. Its upper structure exhibits the Second Empire style elements of a mansard roof on the central tower and iron cresting on the roof. The Classical style verandah was a later early 20th century addition.

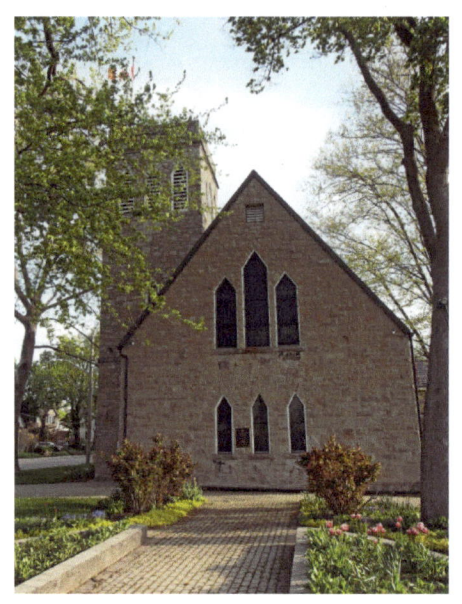

4750 Zimmerman Avenue - Christ Church – Anglican - 1865

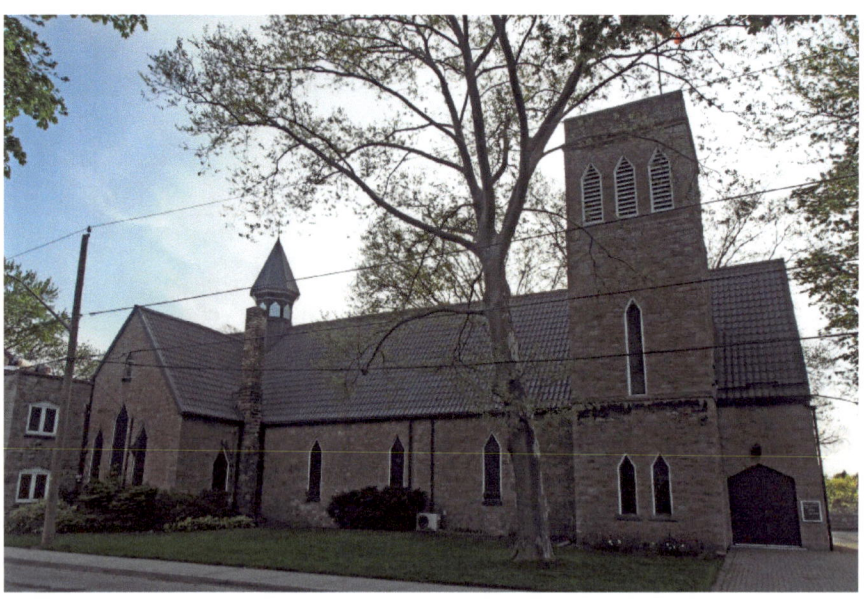

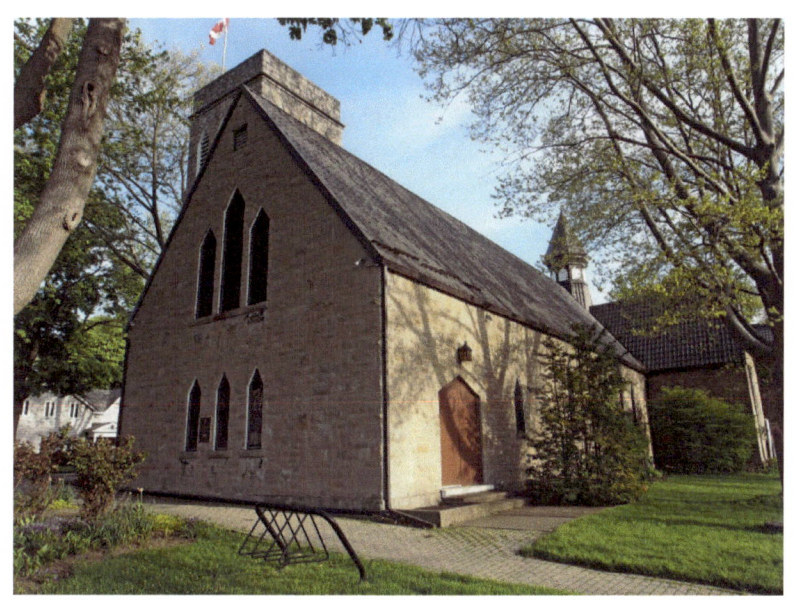

4750 Zimmerman Avenue

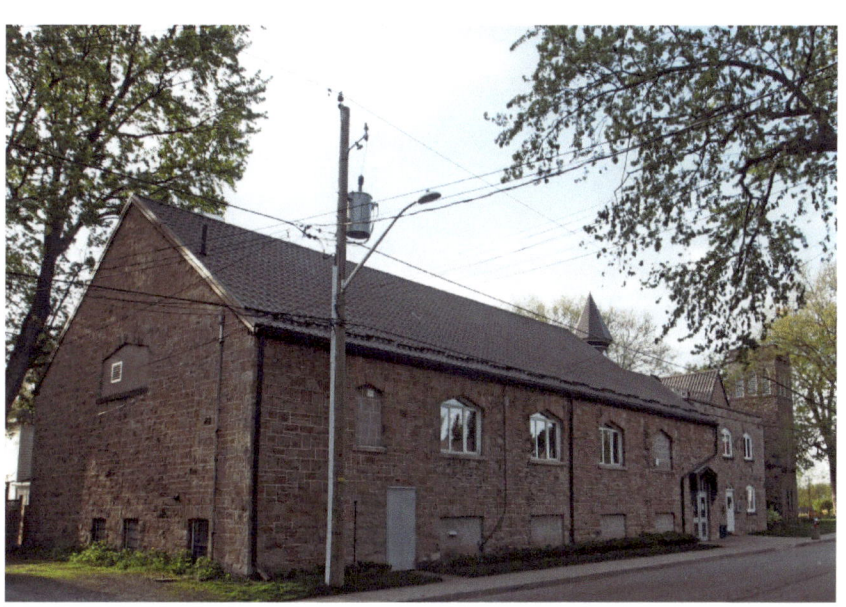

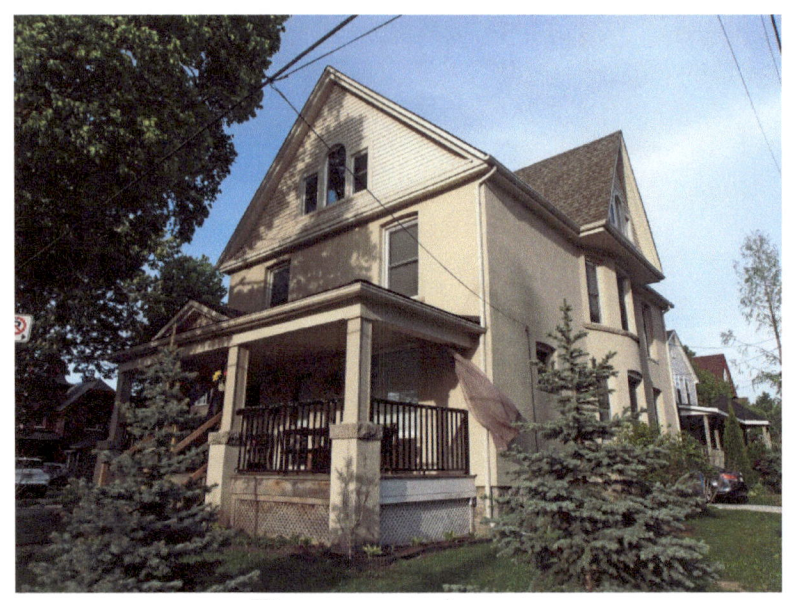

Zimmerman Avenue

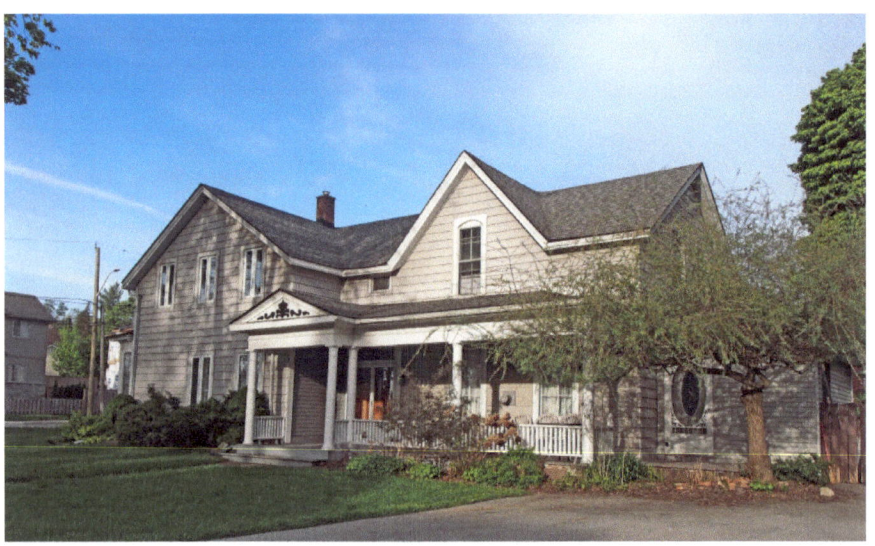

Zimmerman Avenue

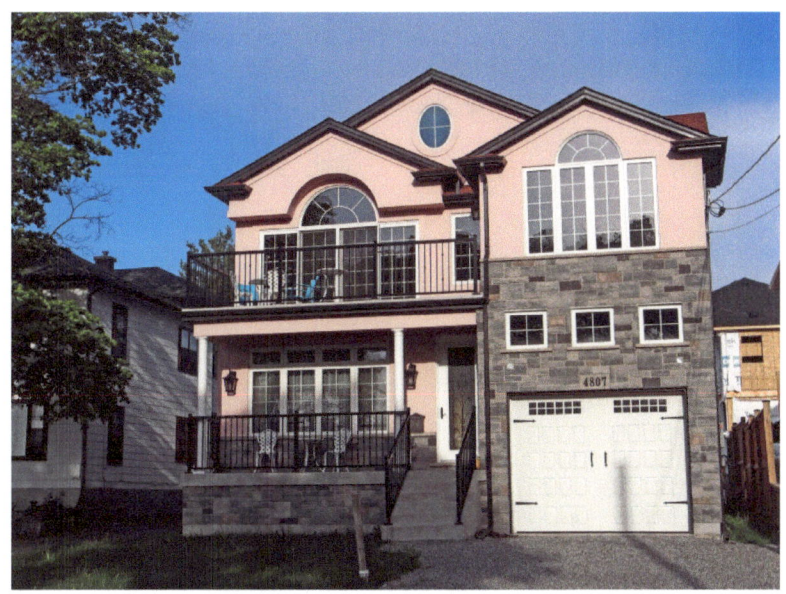

4807 Zimmerman Avenue

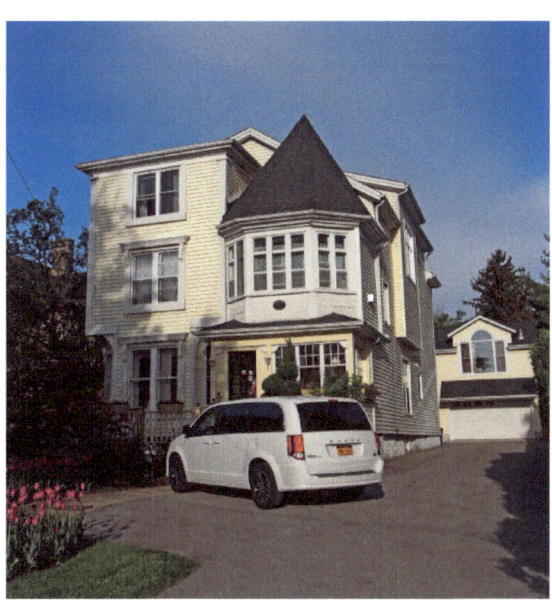

4835 Zimmerman Avenue – Bedham Hall Bed and Breakfast – located on Niagara River two miles from Whirlpool Bridge

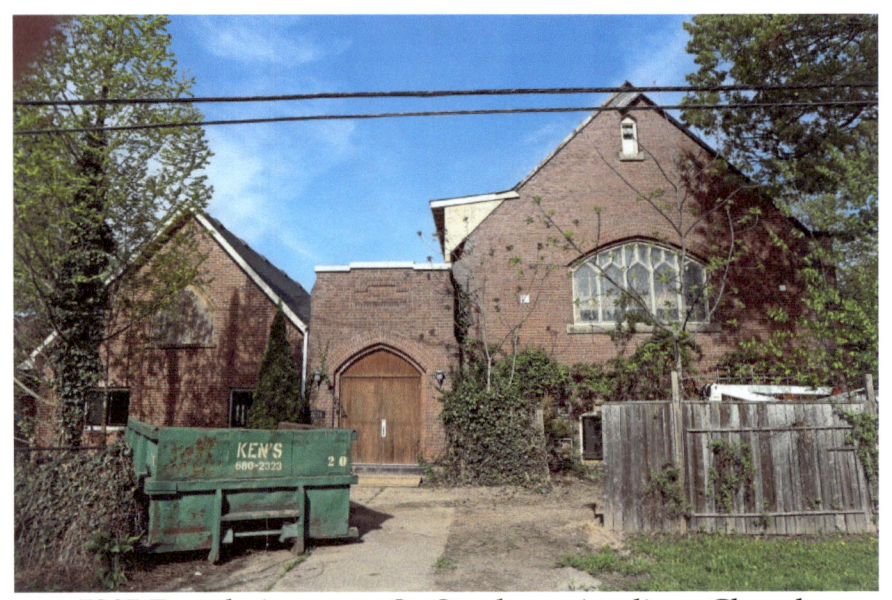

5205 Fourth Avenue - St. Stephens Anglican Church

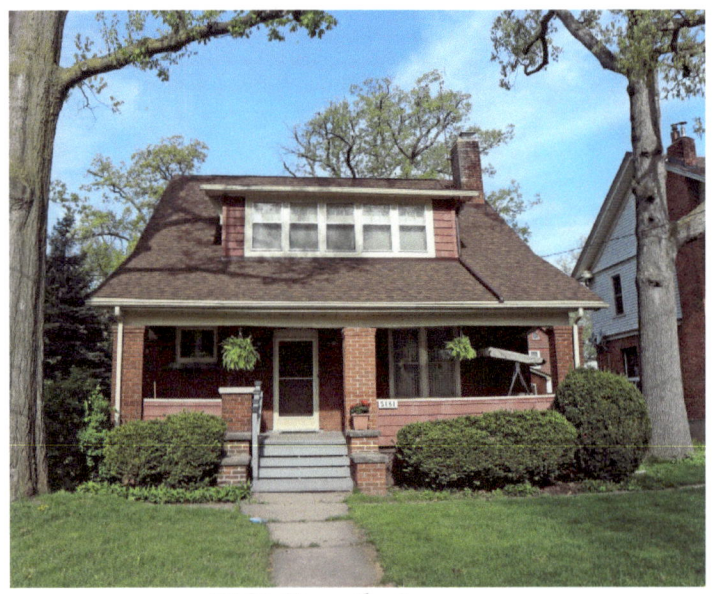

5181 Fourth Avenue

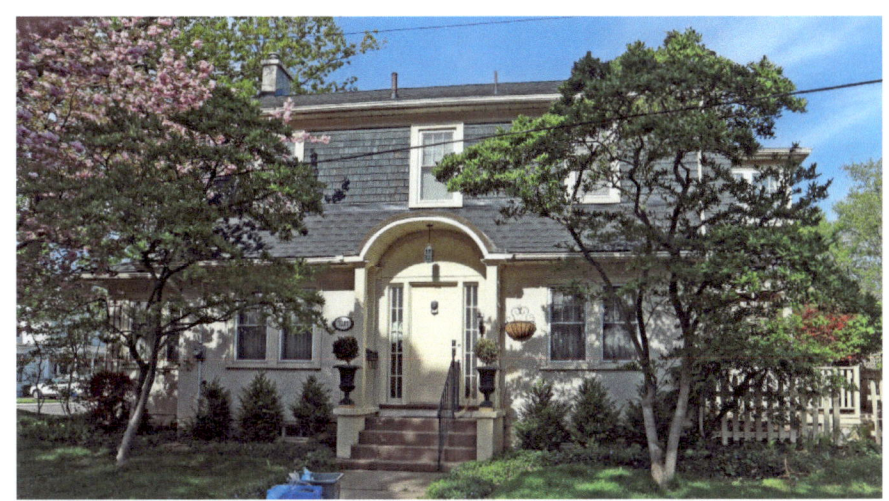

5211 Third Avenue

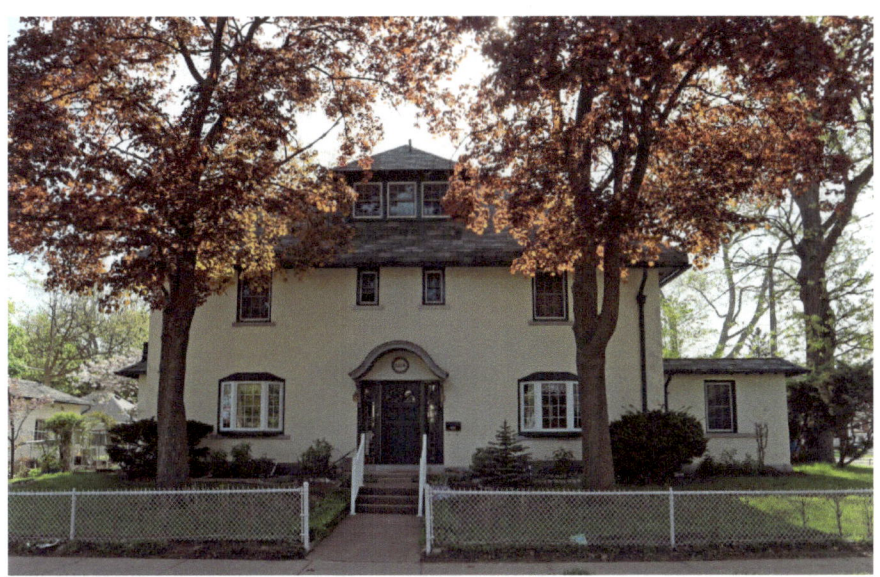

5214 Third Avenue

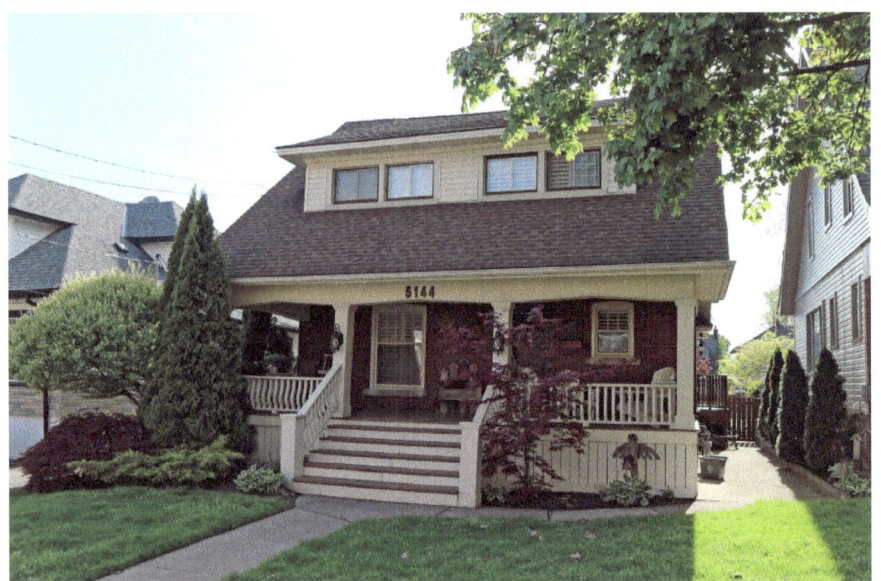

5144 Third Avenue

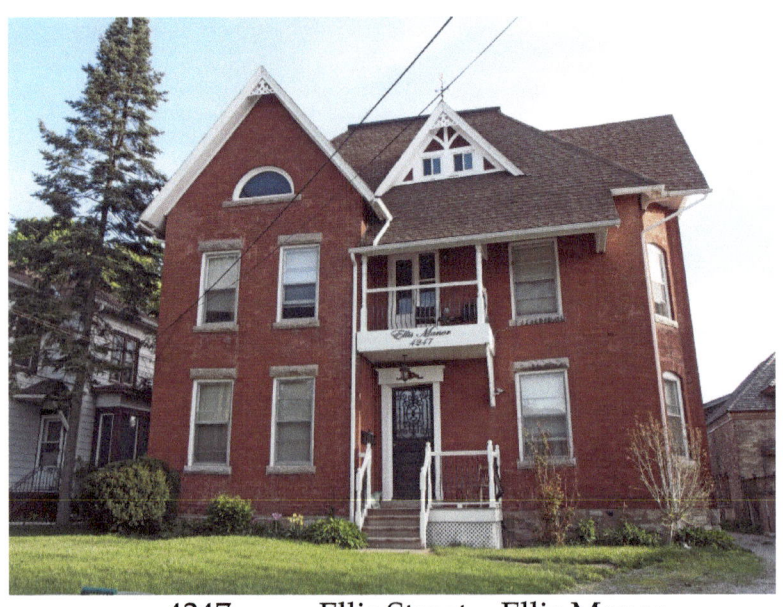

4247　　　Ellis Street – Ellis Manor

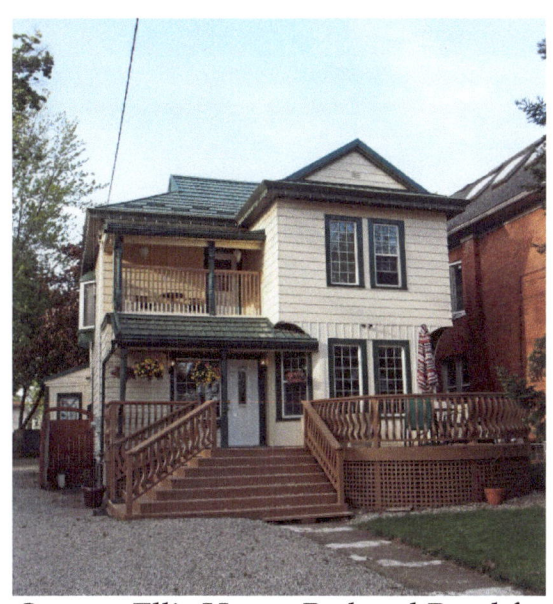

4284 Ellis Street – Ellis House Bed and Breakfast - c. 1847

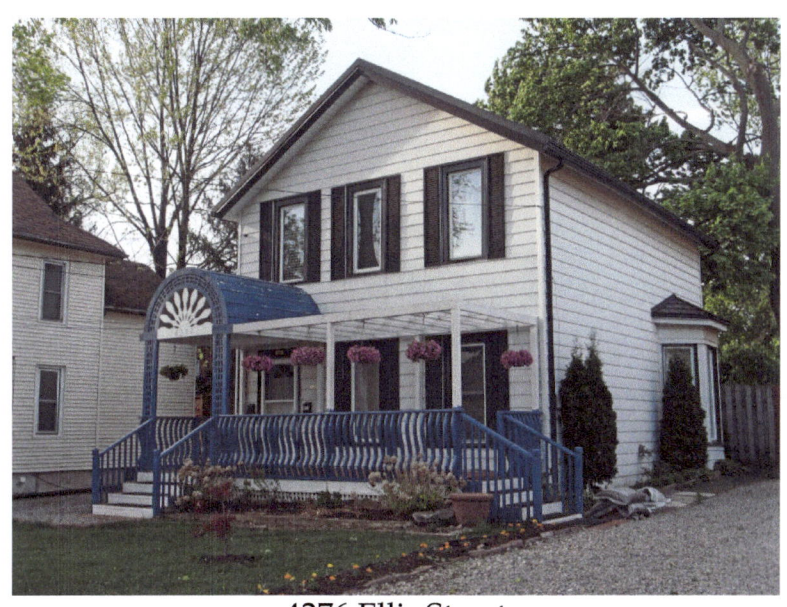

4276 Ellis Street

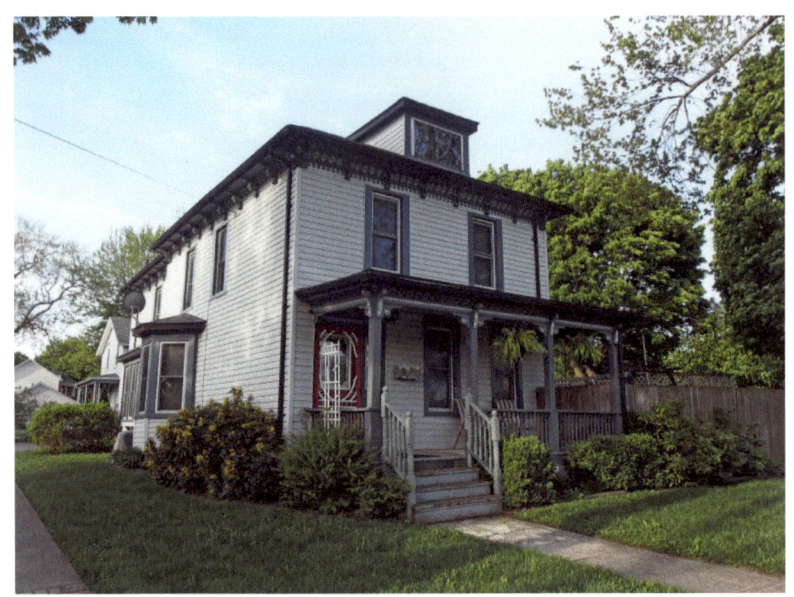

4296 Morrison Street

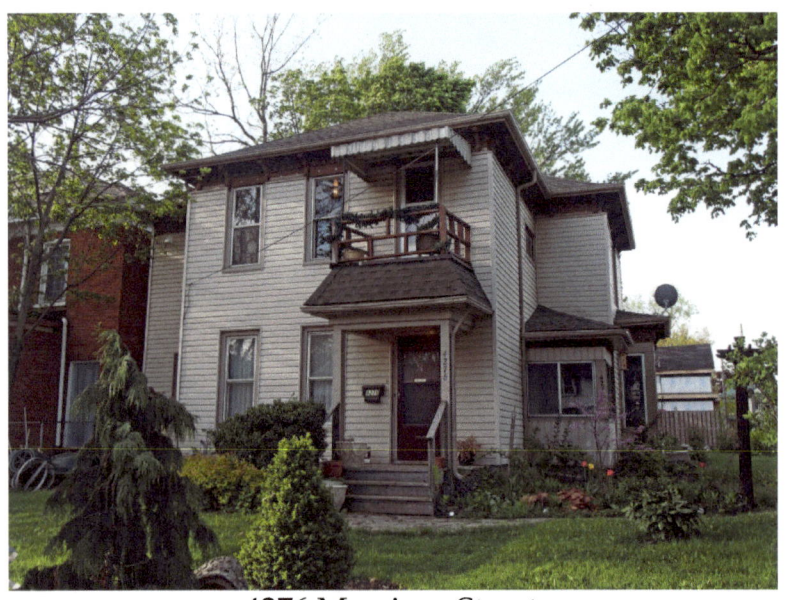

4276 Morrison Street

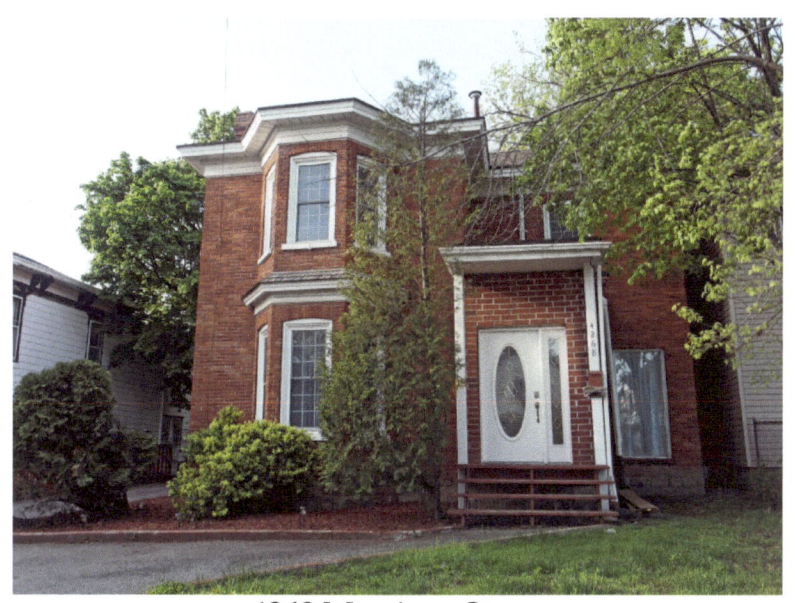

4268 Morrison Street

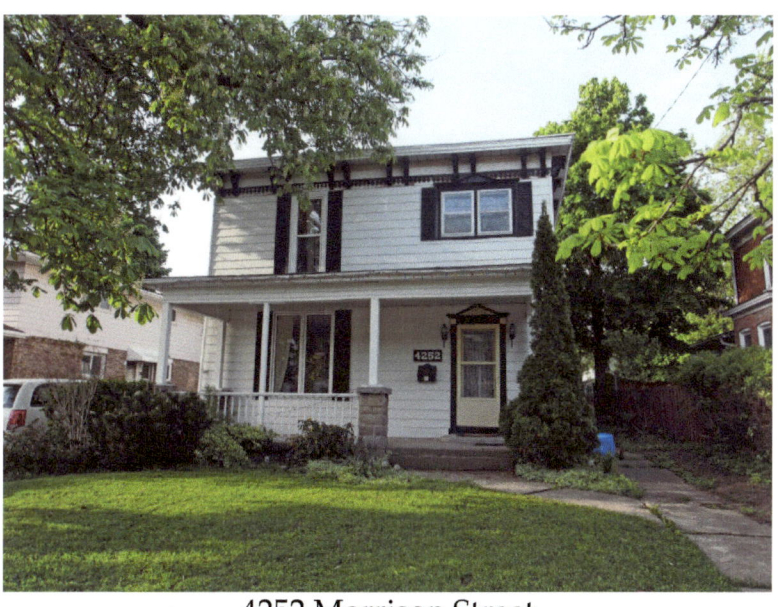

4252 Morrison Street

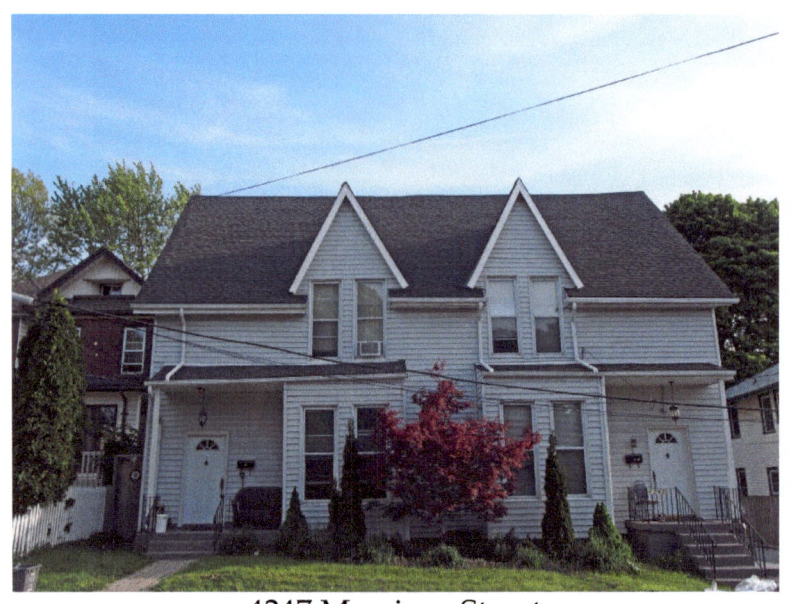

4247 Morrison Street

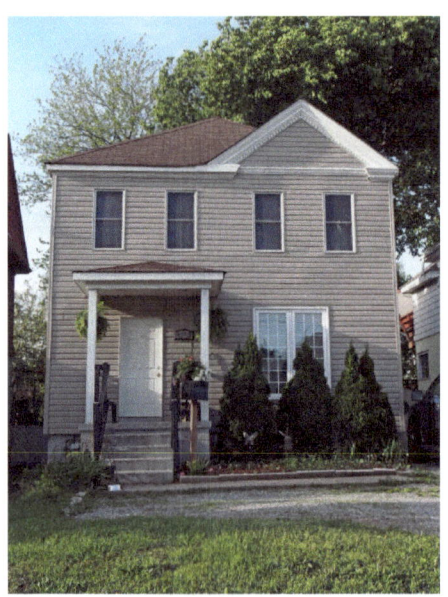

#4252

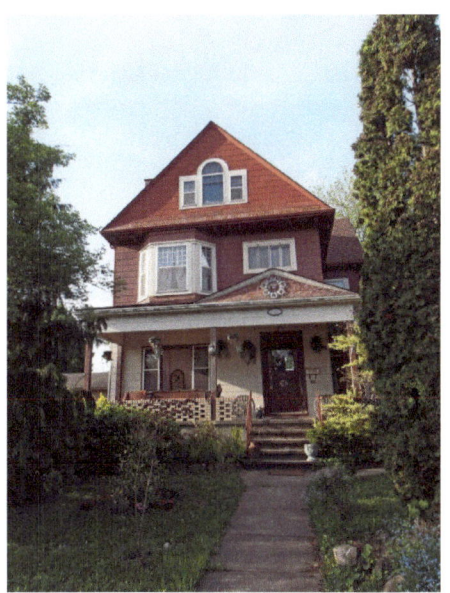

4248 Morrison Street

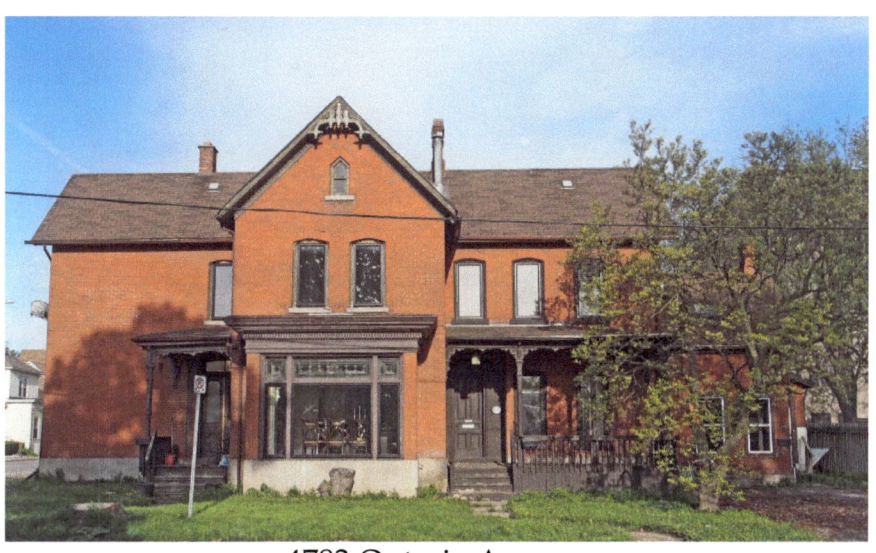

4783 Ontario Avenue

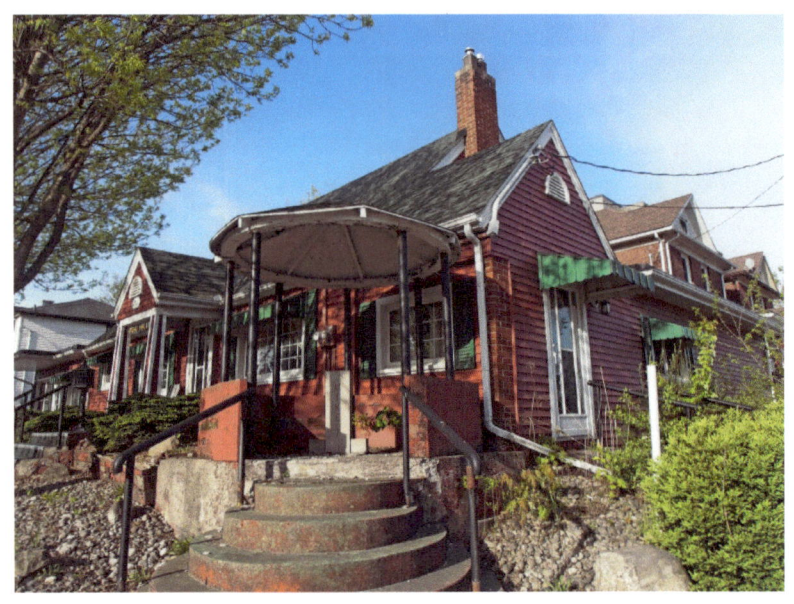

4735 Ontario Avenue – Toad Hall

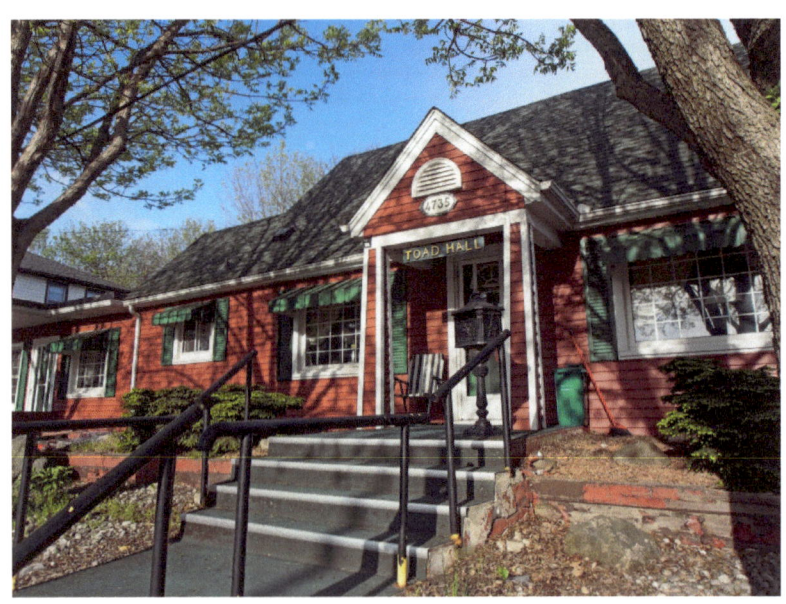

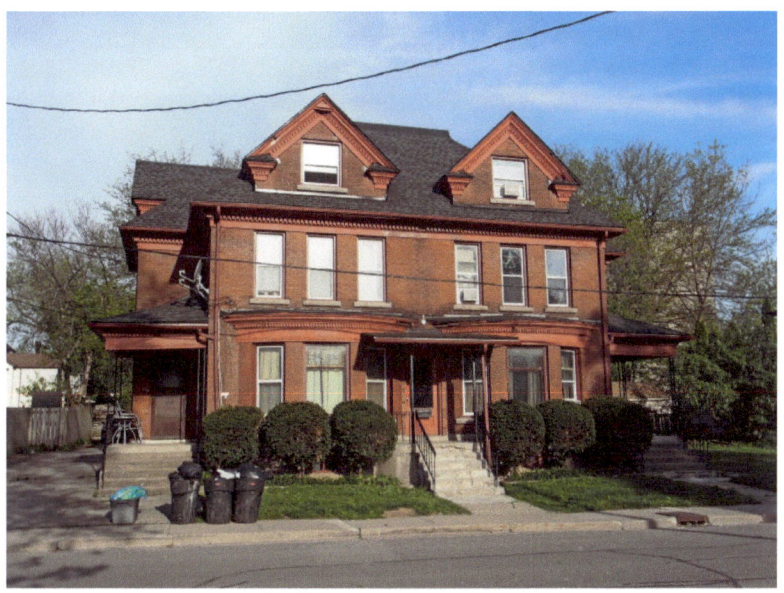

4769 Ontario Avenue

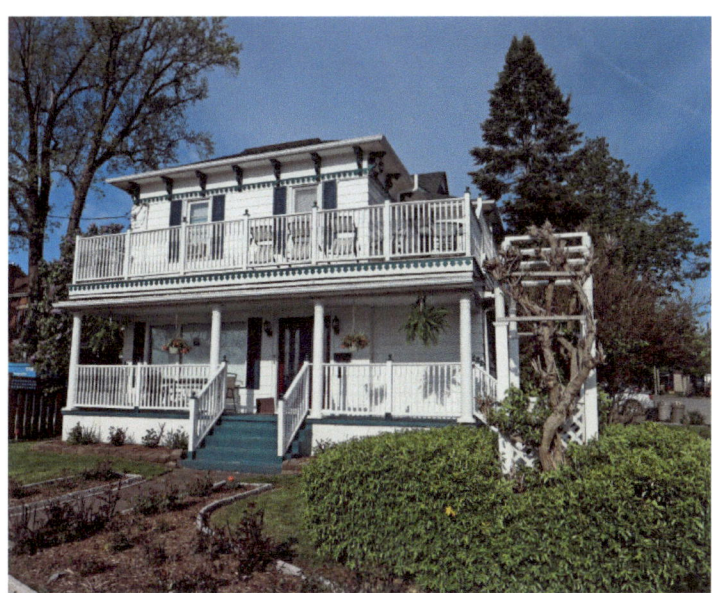

4877 River Road – Bed of Roses Bed and Breakfast

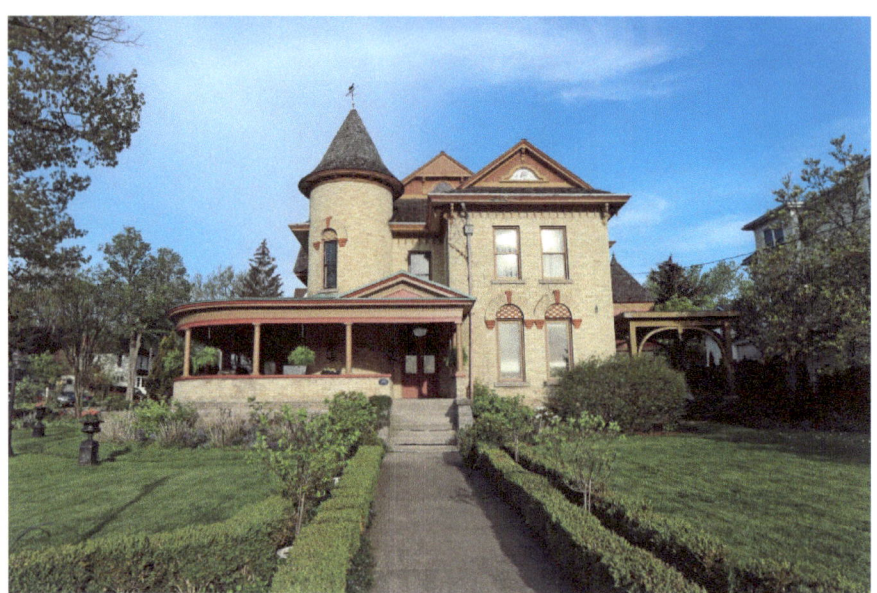

4851 River Road – Doran House – 1886 – Park Place Bed and Breakfast

W.L. Doran and his brother owned the Dominion Suspender Company and Niagara Necktie Factories in town. The house served as an unofficial social club and was the scene of both formal balls and many a wild party.

It is in the Queen Anne Revival style. Built of fine cream colored brick, it has a round corner tower with a conical roof, gable windows of various shapes and a curved verandah with a molded frieze supported by slender columns. To the rear of the house is the original detached coach house.

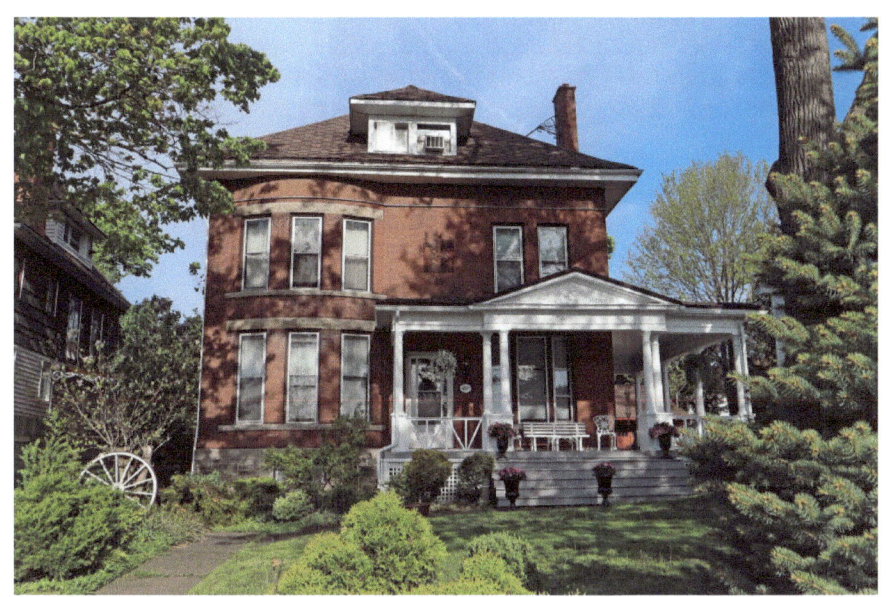

4893 River Road

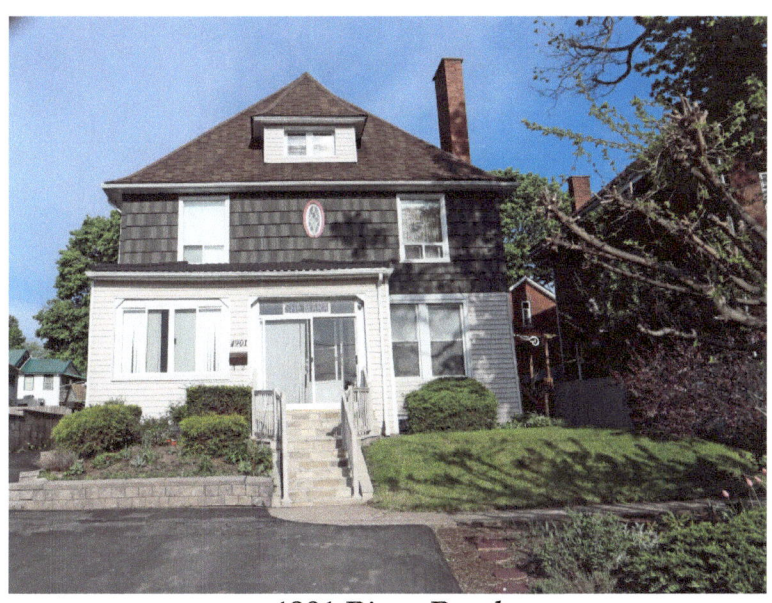

4901 River Road

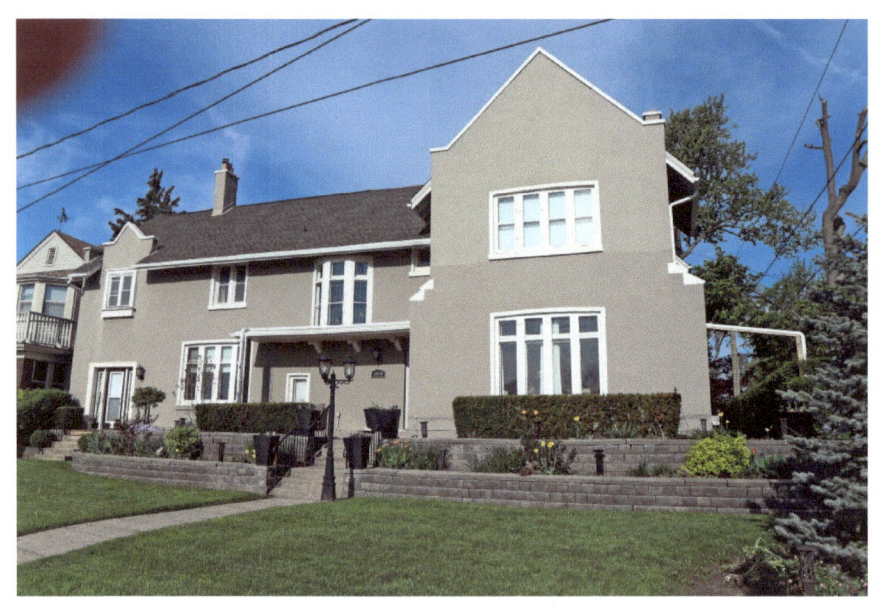

4939 River Road

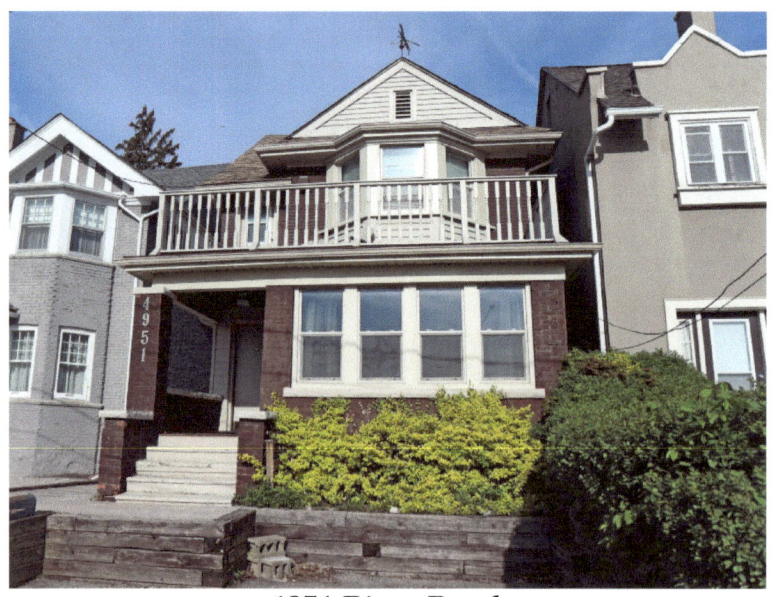

4951 River Road

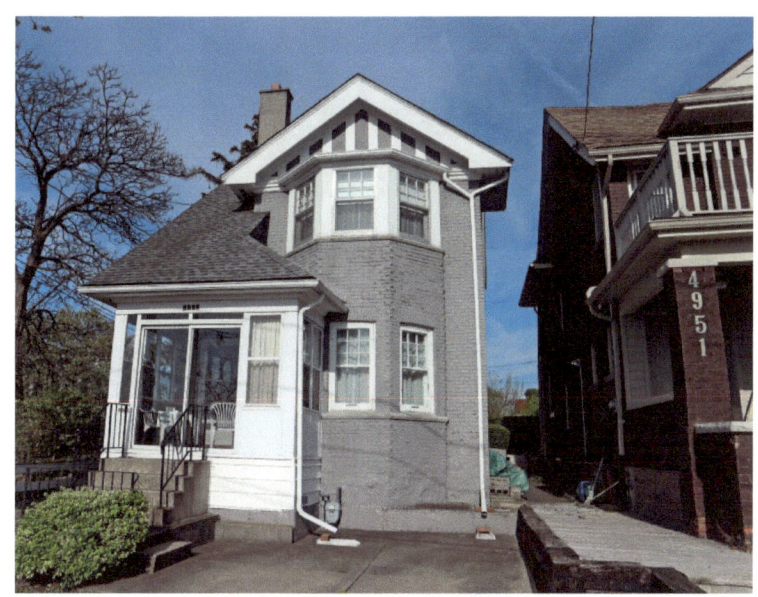

4955 River Road

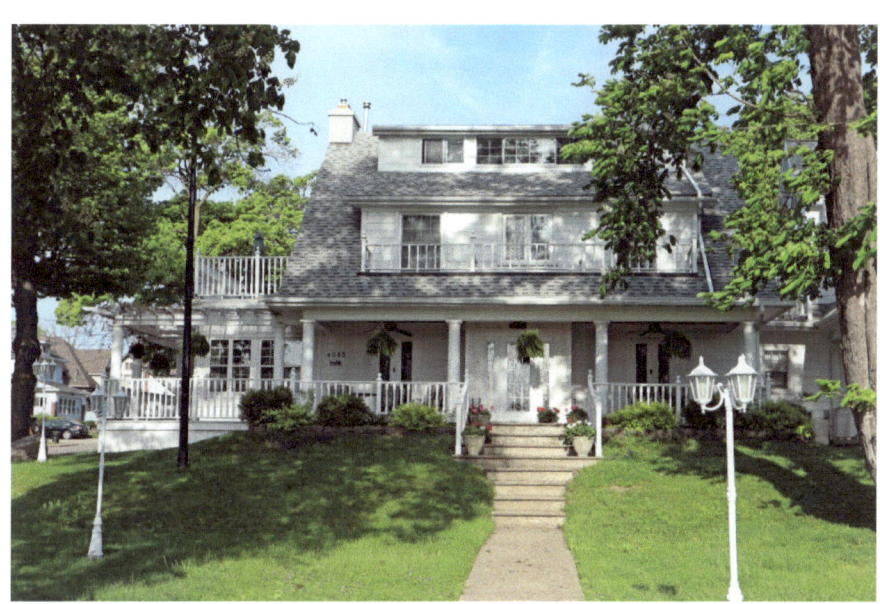

4983 River Road

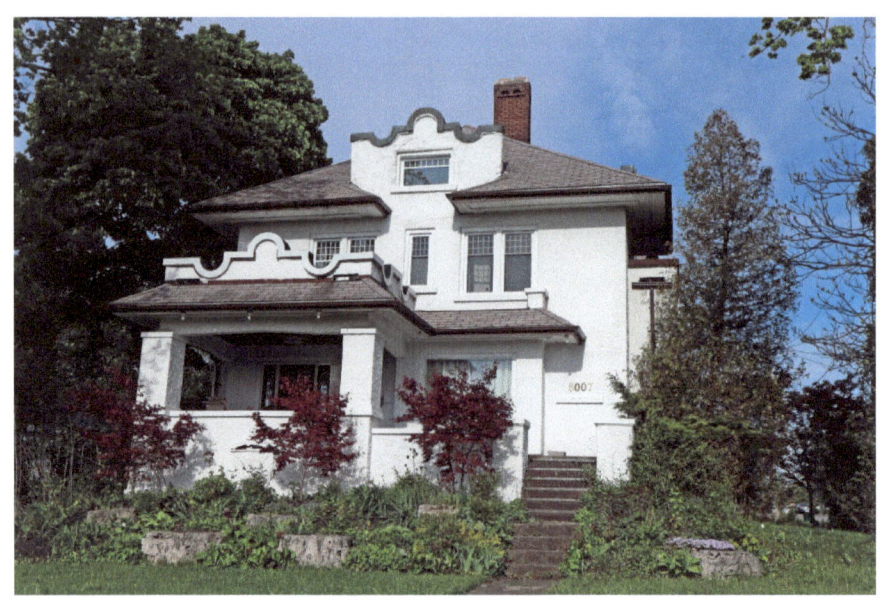

5007 River Road

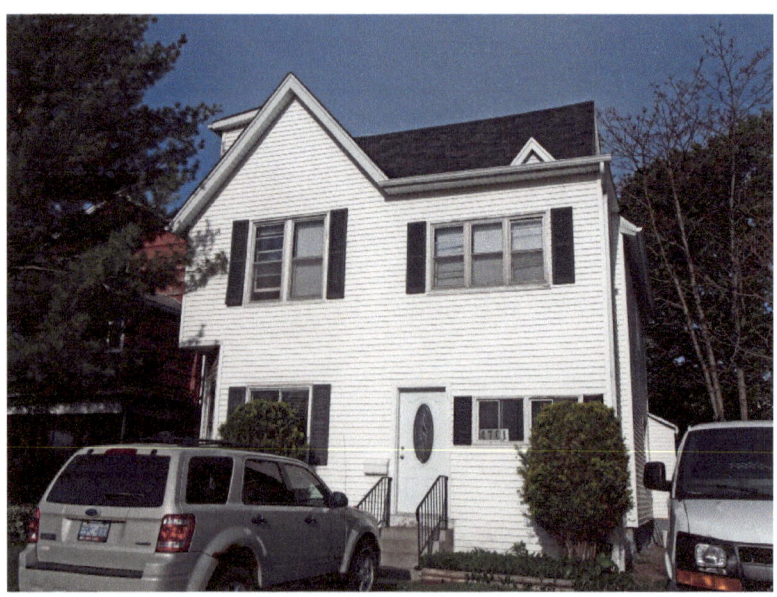

4701 River Road

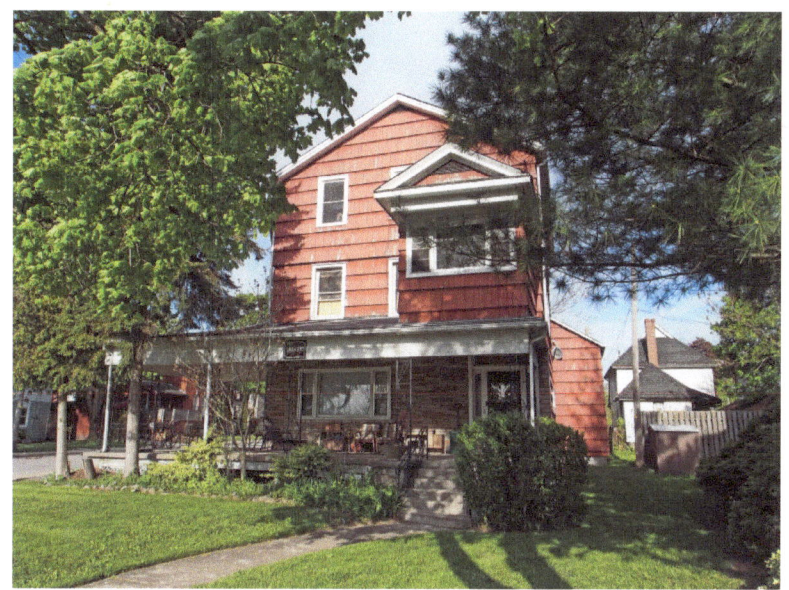

4714 River Road

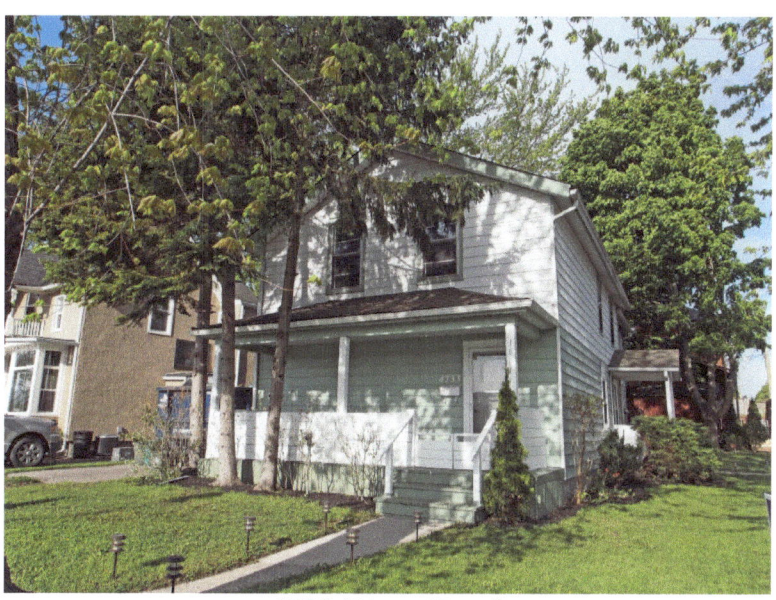

4733 River Road

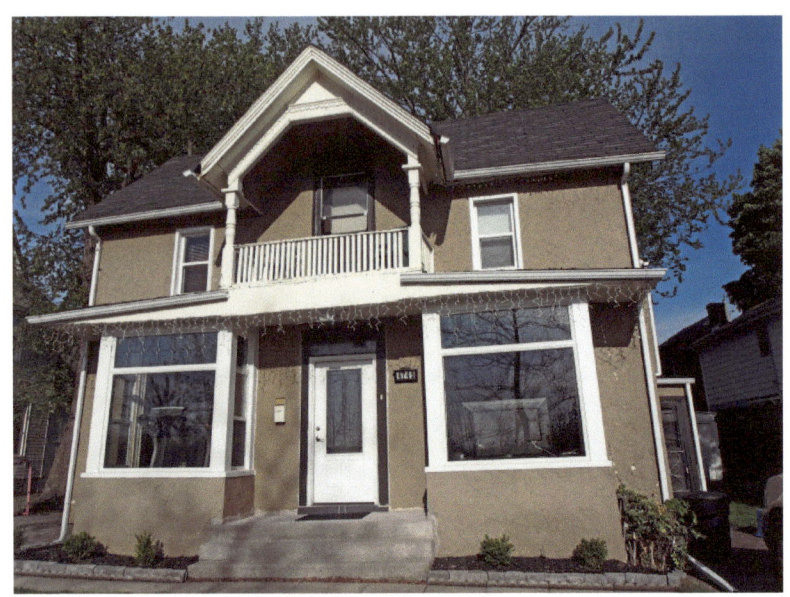

4745 River Road

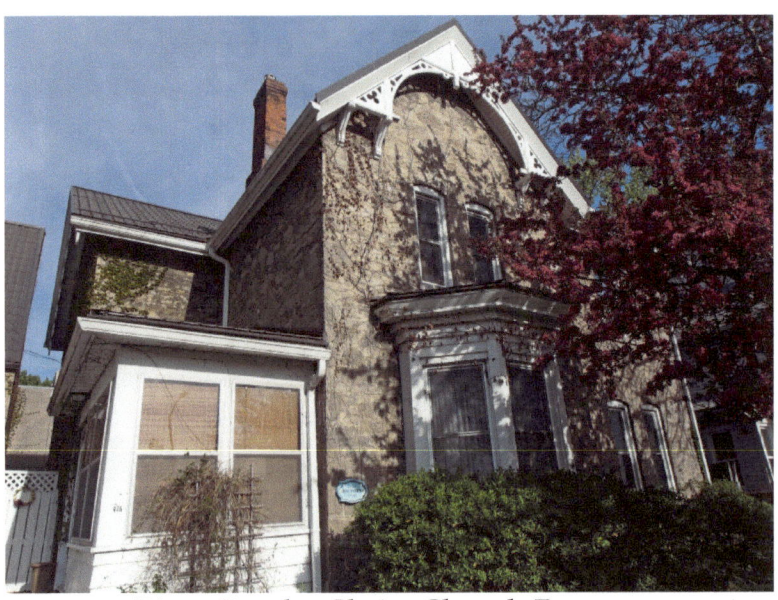

River Road – Christ Church Rectory

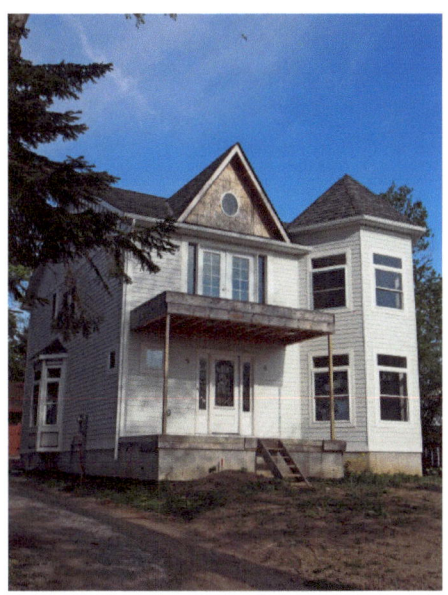

River Road

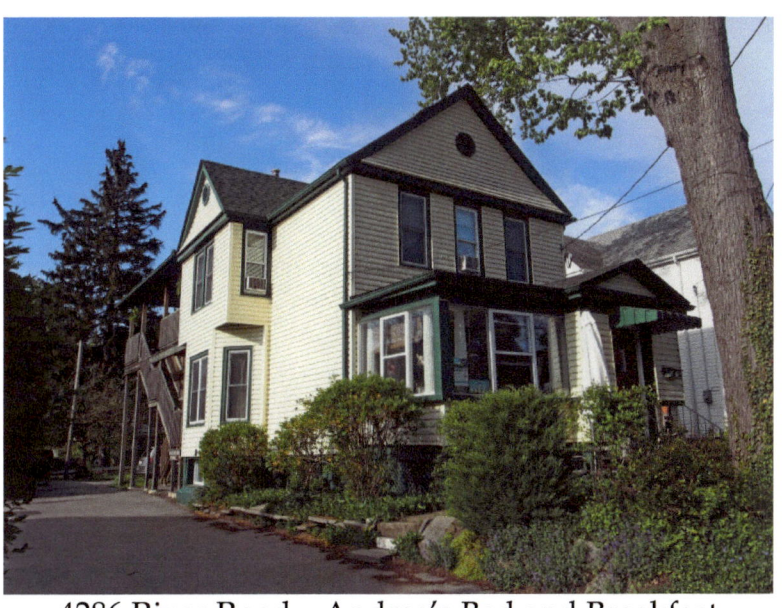

4286 River Road – Andrea's Bed and Breakfast

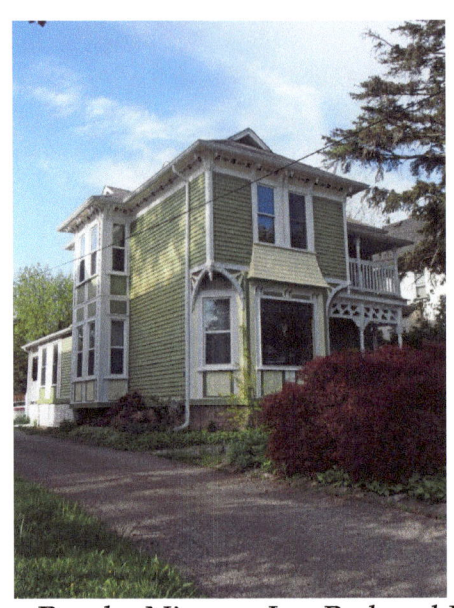

4300 River Road – Niagara Inn Bed and Breakfast

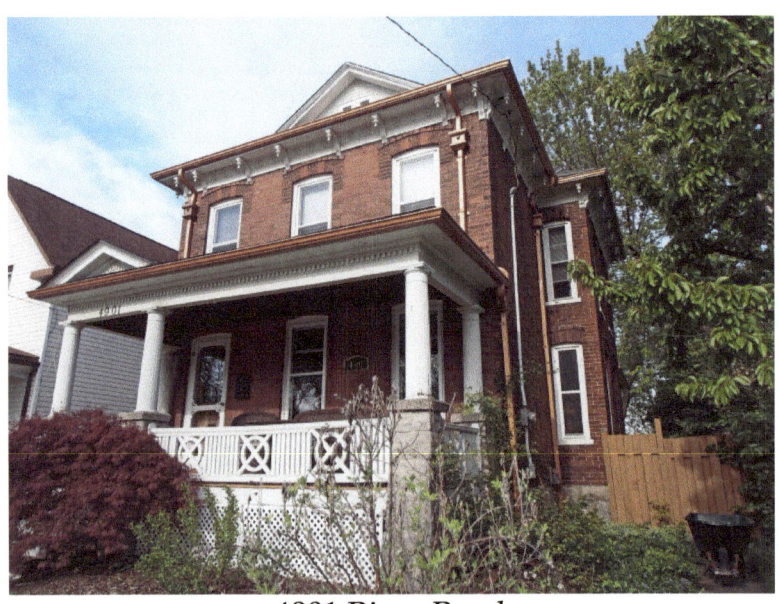

4901 River Road

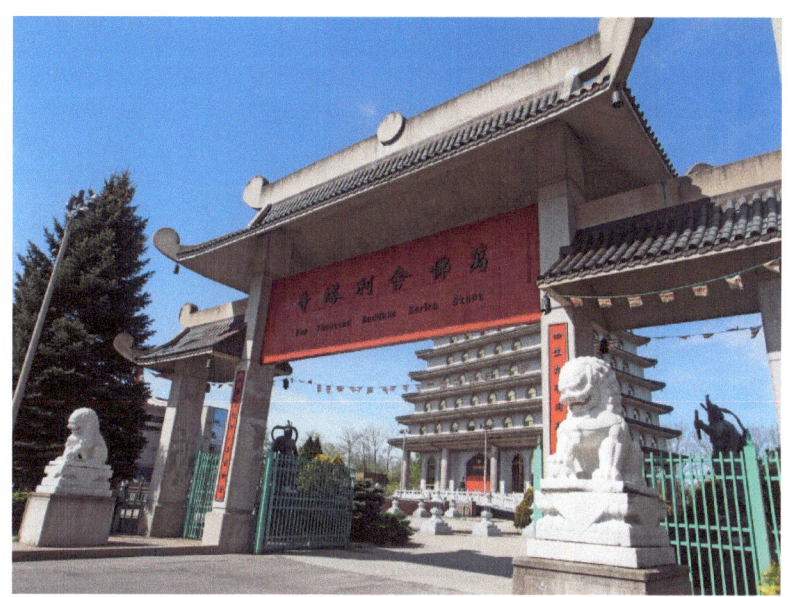

4303 River Road - Namo Amitabha Buddhist Temple

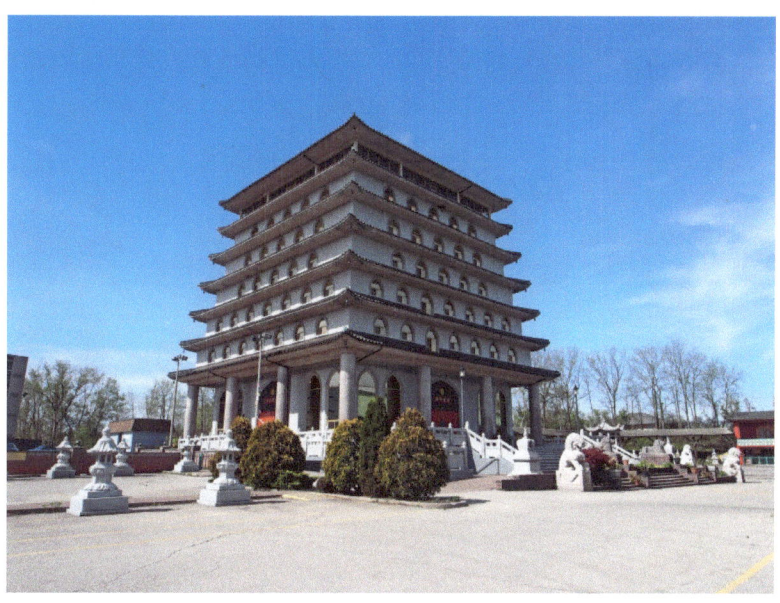

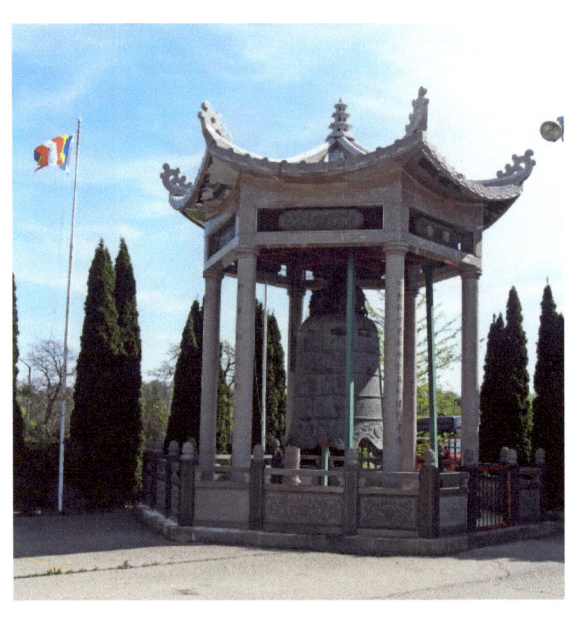

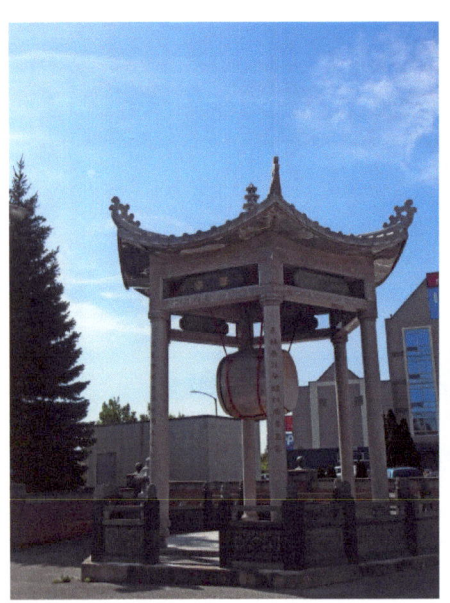
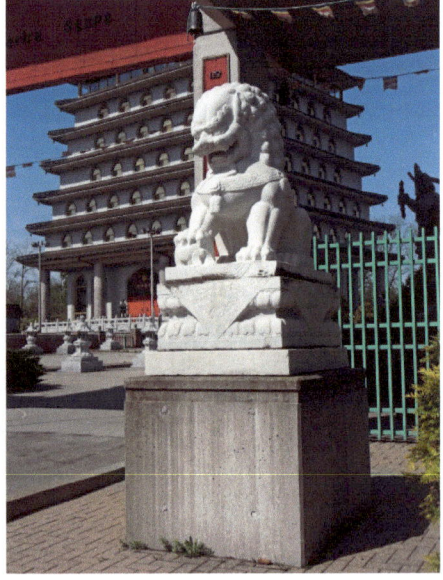

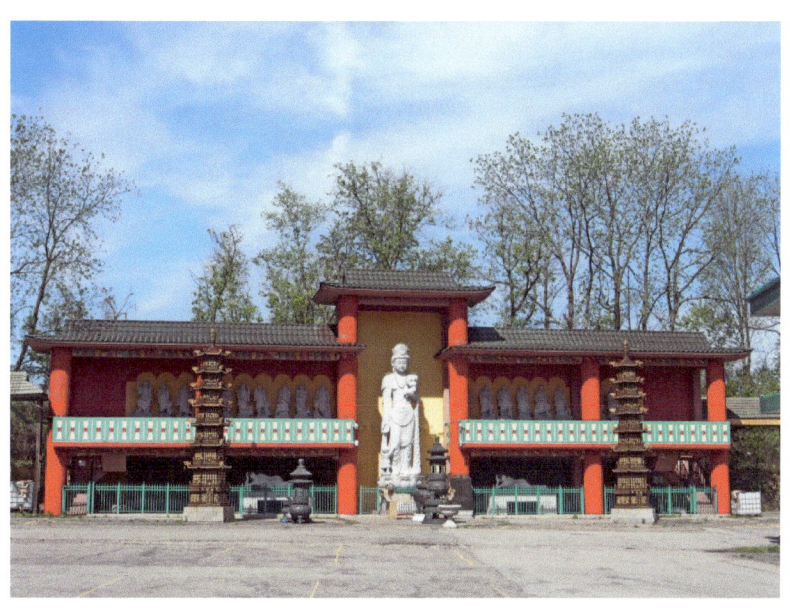

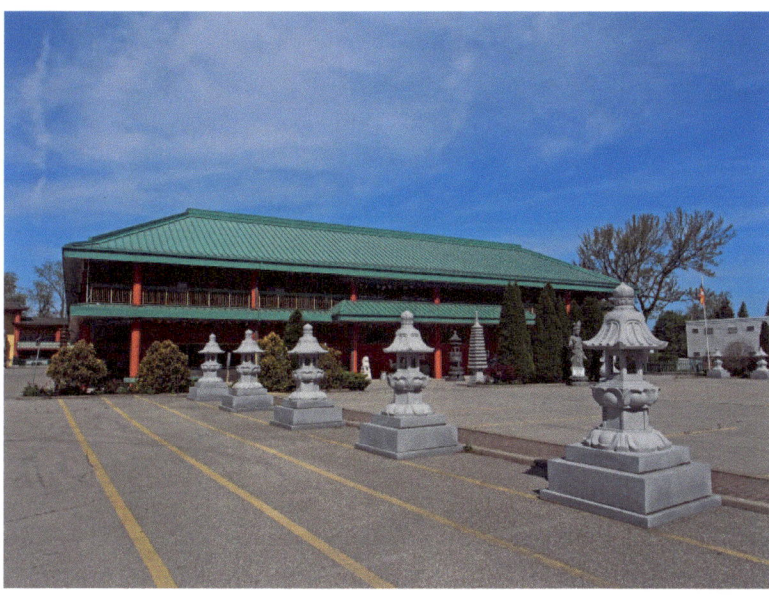

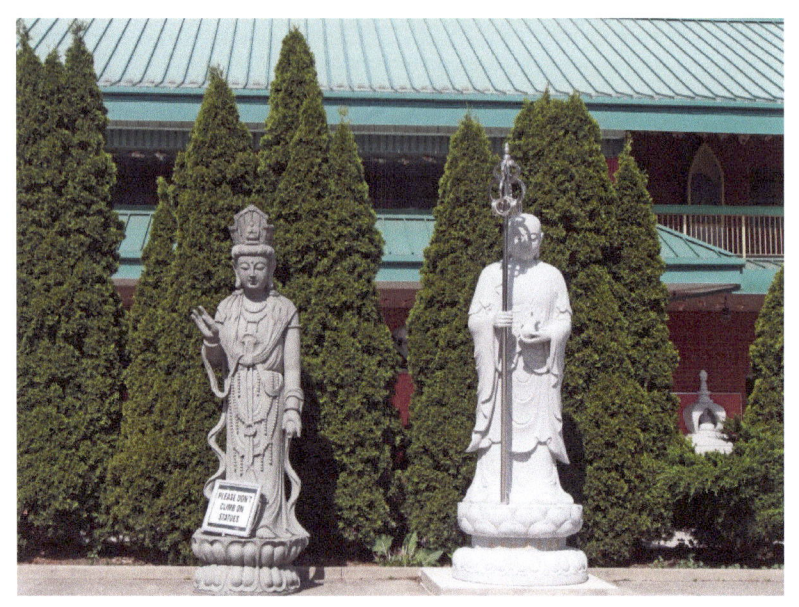

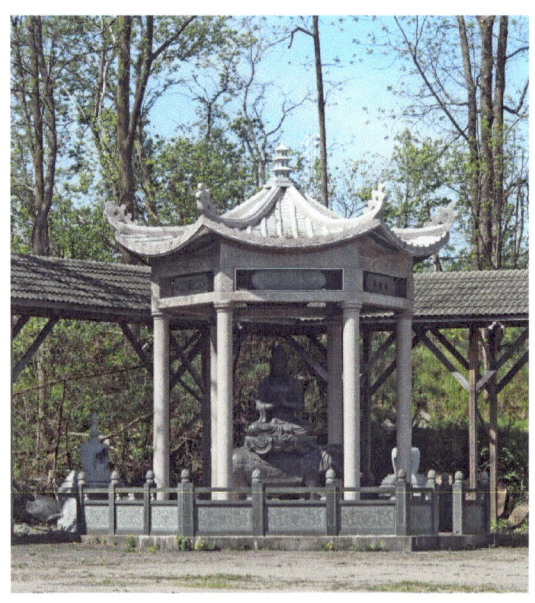

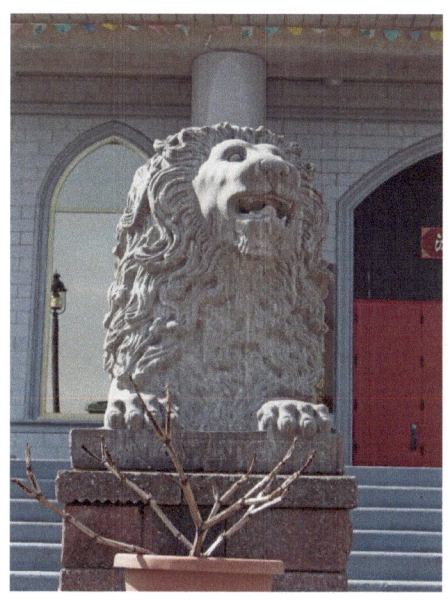
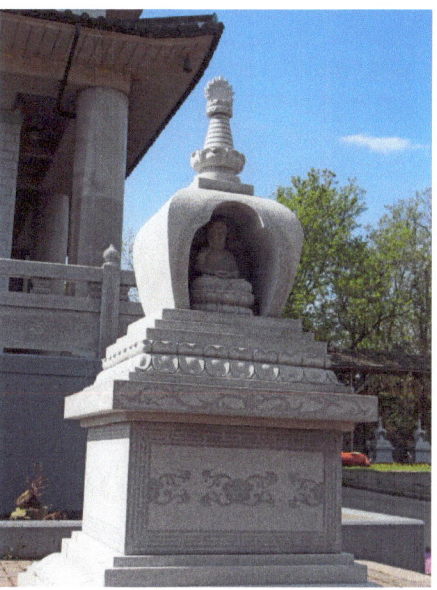
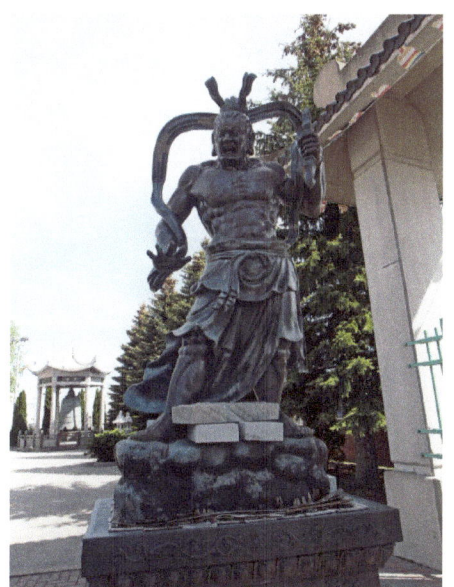
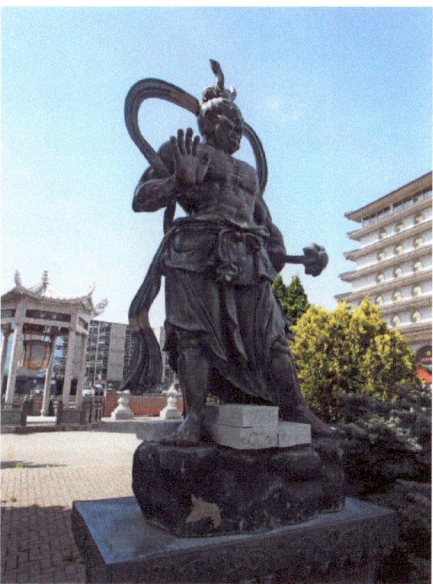

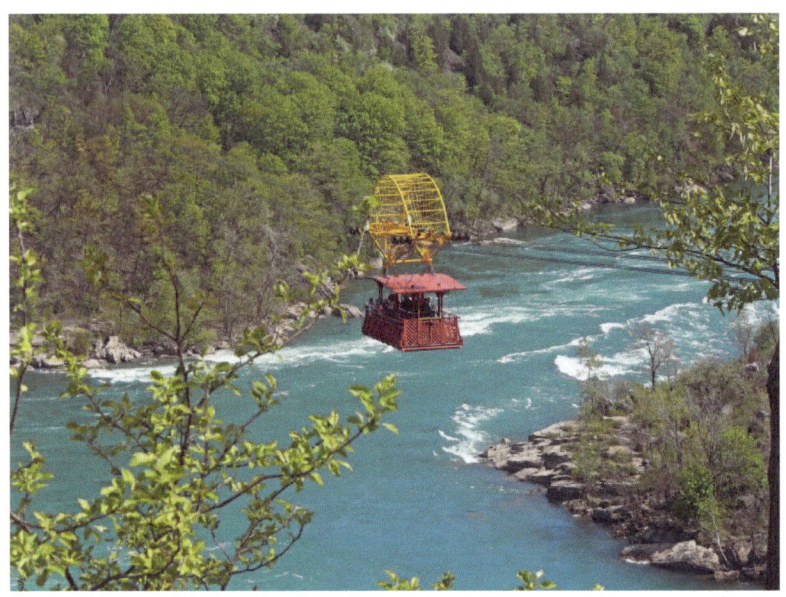

The Niagara Spanish Whirlpool Aero Car was designed by Leonardo Torres Quevedo (1852-1936) and is an example of an innovator and entrepreneur far ahead of his time. It was officially opened on August 8, 1916 and has been gliding continuously over the Niagara River. It is a living testimony to the brilliance of this renowned Spanish engineer.

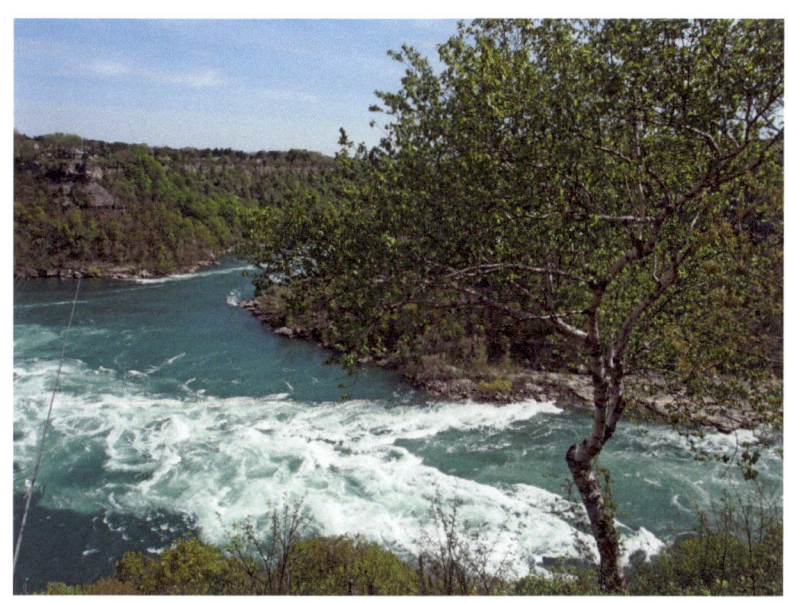

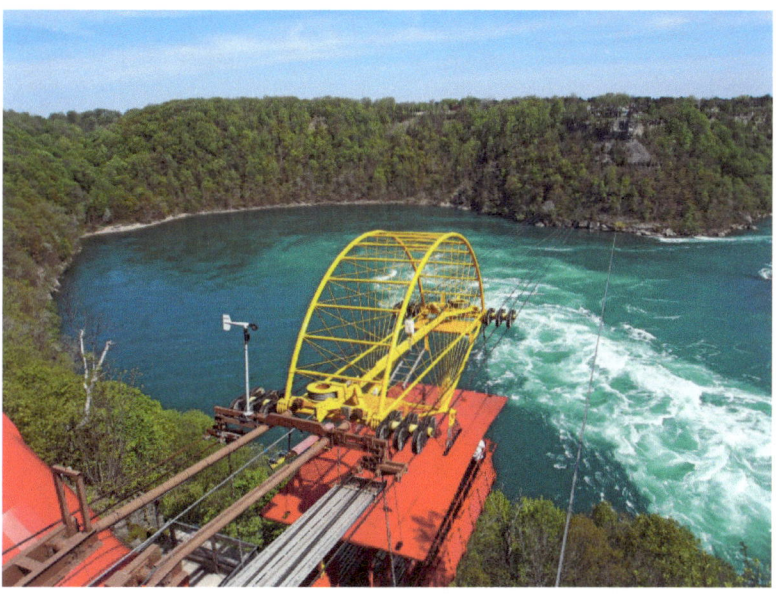

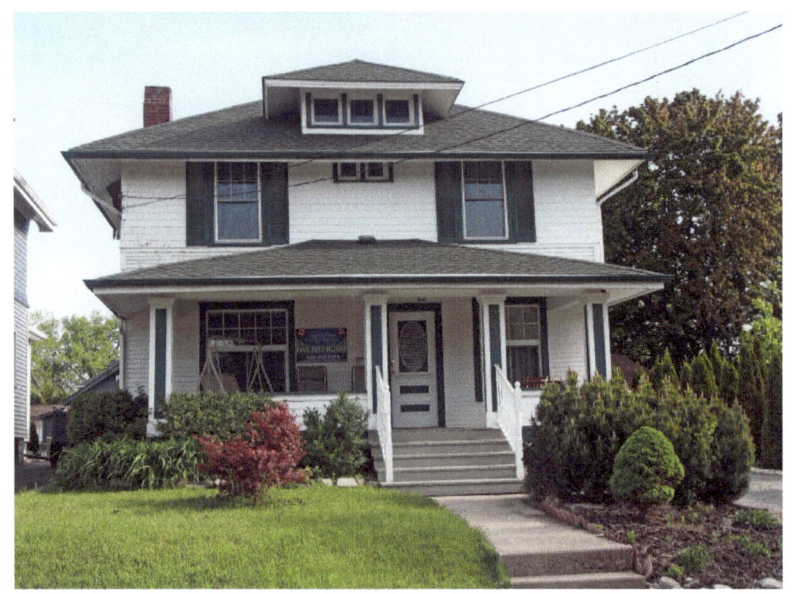
4339 Bampfield Street

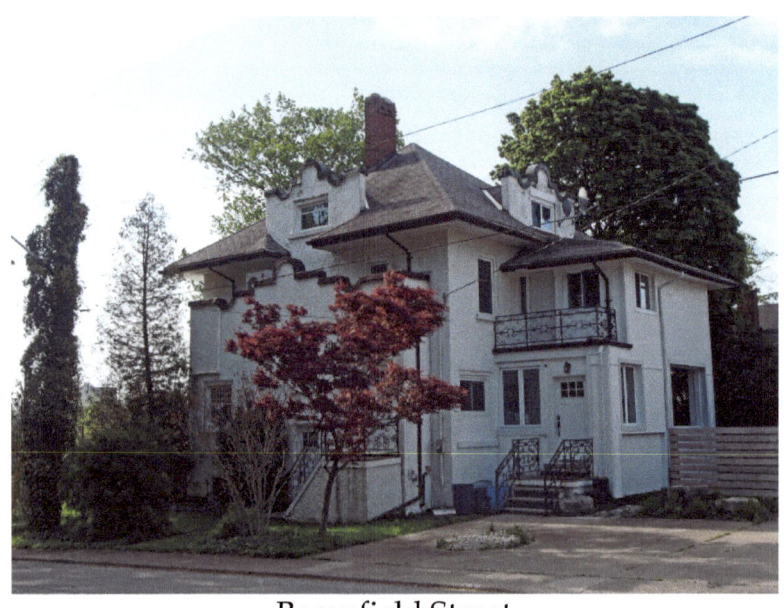
Bampfield Street

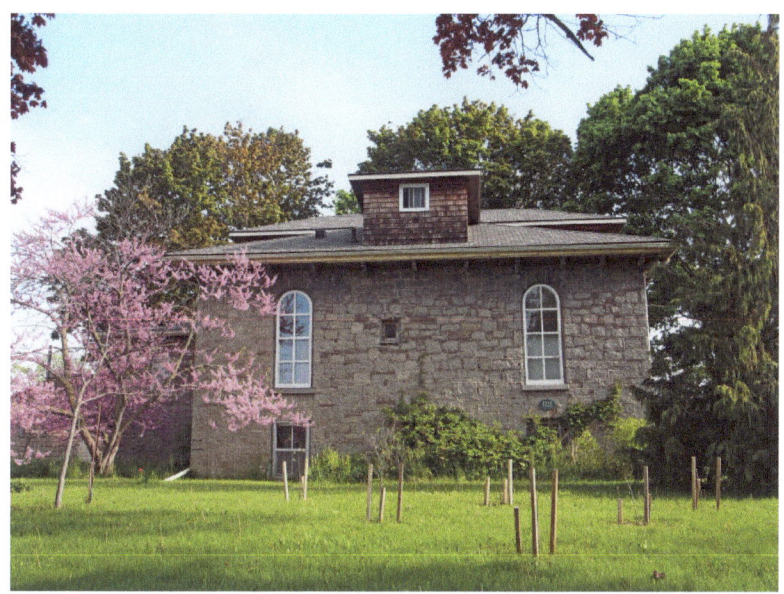

4325 Bampfield Street - Built by local lumber merchant John Merrall, this was the first home of the Bampfield family on their arrival in Clifton in 1860. James Bampfield operated the Great Western Restaurant in the east wing of the railroad station. The house was also reputedly used as a brothel for many years earlier in this century.

The house is a unique variant of the Regency Style with a perfectly square plan, tall limestone block walls and a high raised basement. The basement was dynamited out of the underlying bedrock and built in the earth and rubble technique without mortar. The attached rear porch shed and roof dormers are later additions.

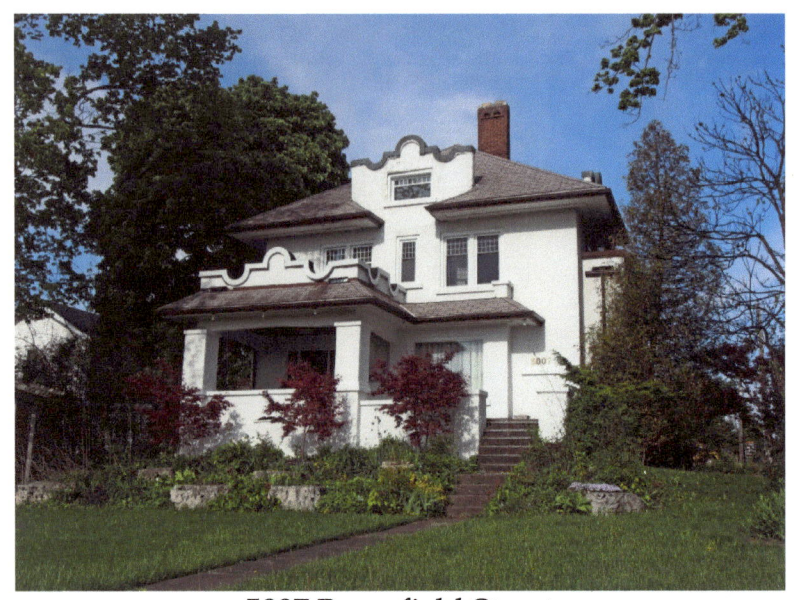

5007 Bampfield Street

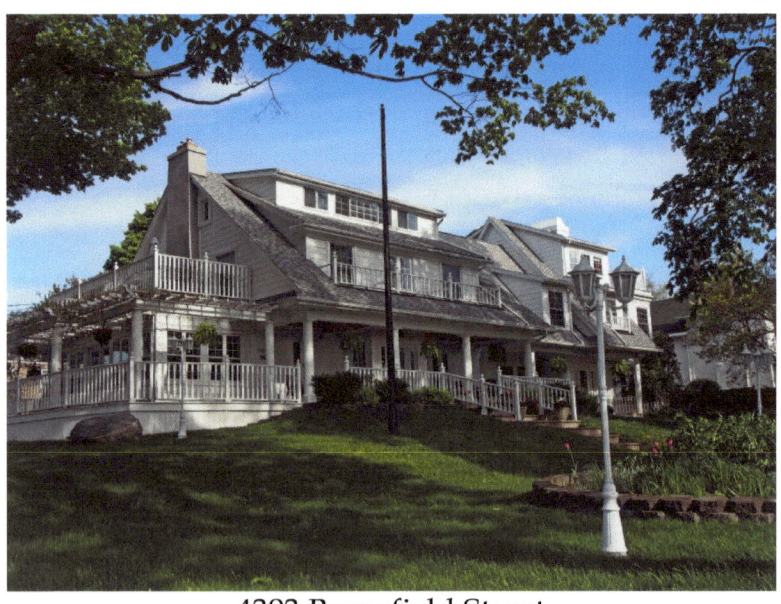

4393 Bampfield Street

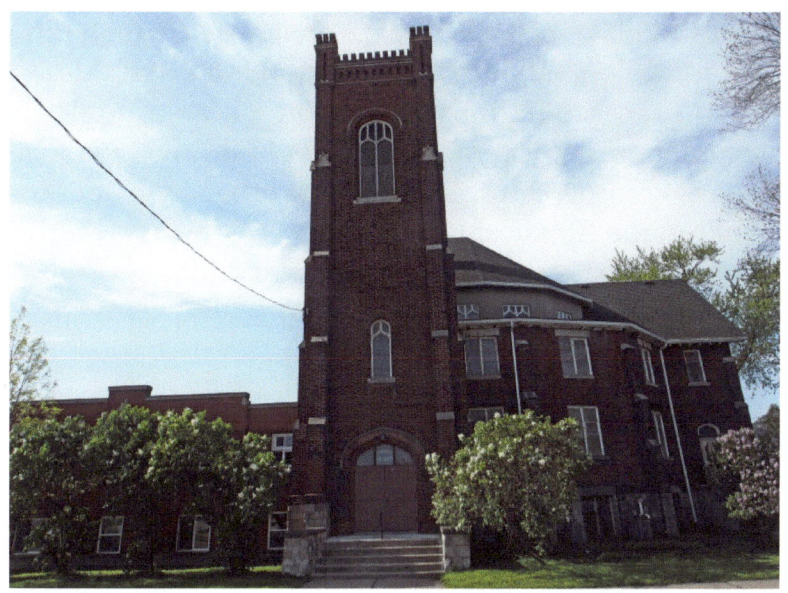

4898 Kitchener Street – Korean Presbyterian Church

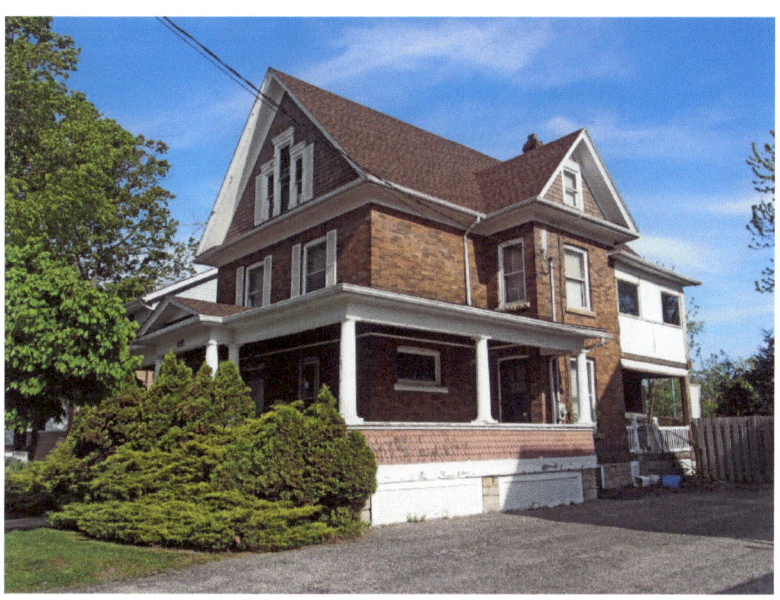

4911 Kitchener Street

# Building Styles

**Classical Revival,** 1820-1860 – This style was an analytical, scientific, and dogmatic revival based on intensive studies of Greek and Roman buildings, concerned with the application of Greek plans and proportions to civic buildings. Schools, libraries, government offices, and most other civic buildings were built in the Classical Revival style. The white columned porches of the Classical Revival domestic buildings are identified with the mansions of wealthy land owners in Canada.

**Edwardian,** 1900-1930 – This style bridges the ornate and elaborate styles of the Victorian era and the simplified styles of the 20$^{th}$ century. Edwardian Classicism provided simple, balanced facades, simple rooflines, dormer windows, large front porches, and smooth brick surfaces. Voussoirs and keystones are used sparingly and are understated. Finials and cresting are absent. Cornice brackets and braces are block-like and openings have flat arches or plain stone lintels.

**Gothic Revival,** 1830-1890 – These decorative buildings have sharply-pitched gables with highly detailed verge boards, pointed-arch window openings, and dichromatic brickwork. It is a common style in Ontario.

**Neo-Classical,** 1810-1850 – This style was a direct result of the War of 1812. Many Upper Canadians returning from the war with the United States were second or third generation Loyalists who had inherited land and means from their forefathers. Once the conflict had passed, they had the money and the time to expand their holdings and indulge their architectural whims. Both residential and commercial buildings were constructed on the traditional Georgian plan, but they had a new gaiety and light-heartedness. Detailing became more refined, delicate, and elegant.

**Queen Anne**, 1885-1900 – This style is distinguished by an irregular outline featuring a combination of an offset tower, broad gables, projecting two-story bays, verandahs, multi-sloped roofs, and tall, decorative chimneys. A mixture of brick and wood is common. Windows often have one large single-paned bottom sash and small panes in the upper sash.

**Regency Style,** 1811-1820: Numerous towns and cities enjoy elegant rows of terraced houses built in what is now called the Regency Style. Windows are tall and thin, with very small glazing bars separating the panes of glass. Balconies are of extremely fine ironwork, made of such delicate curves as to seem almost too frail to support the structure. Proportions are kept simple, relying on clean, classical lines for effect rather than decorative touches. Windows and doors, particularly those on the ground floors, are often round-headed. Curved bow windows are popular, and detached villas often featured garden windows extending right down to the ground.

# Other Books by Barbara Raue

Coins of Gold
Arrows, Indians and Love
The Life and Times of Barbara
The Cromwell Family Book
Laura Secord Discovered
Daddy Where Are You?

Montana Series
Book 1: Montana Dream
Book 2: Life on the Montana Frontier
Book 3: Montana to Boston and Back
Book 4: Montana Sons Go to War
Book 5: Montana Sons Return from War

Donaldson Series
Book 1: Rite of Passage
Book 2: Rite of Marriage

Barbara is The Authority on Saving Our History One Photo at a Time. She is pursuing her interest in photography and architecture by preserving a record through photos of old buildings from the 1800s and 1900s with their unique architecture. Enjoy the beautiful architecture in the comfort of your living room. Dream about what it was like in those by-gone days. Dream about what it was like to live in a mansion like one of those in this book.

Barbara Raue, a wife, mother and grandmother, is an avid reader and writer. She has researched and compiled several family histories. In 2010, Barbara published her book "Coins of Gold," which celebrates the courageous life of her mother, May Todd. Barbara's second book is a historical fiction "Arrows, Indians and Love" which takes place in Boonesborough, Kentucky during the time of Daniel Boone. In 2013, Barbara published *The Cromwell Family Book* in which she traces her ancestry generations back into Great Britain. Her second novel is called *Laura Secord Discovered,* in which the story of Laura's service during the War of 1812 is shared. Barbara's memoir is titled *Daddy Where Are You?* It tells of her life growing up without a father. Five novels in the Montana Series have been published, *Montana Dream, Life on the Montana Frontier, Montana to Boston and Back, Montana Sons Go to War,* and *Montana Sons Return from War.* The Donaldson series of two novels is available: *Rite of Passage* and *Rite of Marriage.*

This is a link to Barbara's website to view all of her books
http://barbararaue.ca

www.ingramcontent.com/pod-product-compliance
Lightning Source LLC
Chambersburg PA
CBHW041941240526
45473CB00033B/174